TRADITIONAL
SWEDISH COOKING

CAROLINE HOFBERG

TRADITIONAL SWEDISH COOKING

Translation by Monika Romare

Skyhorse Publishing

www.skyhorsepublishing.com

10 9 8 7 6 5 4 3 2 1

Library of Congress Cataloging-in-Publication Data is available on file.
ISBN: 978-1-61608-136-2

Printed in China

CONTENTS

I have a treasure: my grandmother's cookbooks. Until recently, they were safely stored in a treasure chest: my closet. A big package wrapped in brown paper. Originally they were just simple black notebooks. Blank pages that my grandmother turned into a piece of food history.

There are many reasons why I haven't opened the package until now. One was that I never imagined the contents would be as extensive as they turned out to be. The entire time, I thought they were just simple books with a few of her favorite recipes, the same way I collect mine—cut and pasted or scribbled down. They are valuable to me, of course, but barely to anybody else.

I was completely captivated by the piece of history that I uncovered about a woman and her passion for food. My grandmother was a very artistic woman. In her own way she collected everything from recipes to practical tips, advice on bookkeeping in the home, and life stories. All in little black notebooks. Decade after decade.

I am proud and touched by it. At the same time, I am concerned with how to preserve our traditional Swedish food culture while allowing it to develop with the exotic influences that our current times give us access to. We need to remember our own kitchen with its produce from the sea, the forest, the lakes, and the gardens. Herbs and spices such as dill, horseradish, honey, and juniper berries. Not to mention rapeseed oil and butter, which make the flavors bloom. Swedish home-cooked meals are influenced by what our forests have to offer. Lingonberries, blueberries, cloudberries, and mushrooms. We are able to enjoy fish and seafood from cold-water streams. Fruits and vegetables that have ripened slowly and acquired intense flavors. It is a truly inspiring and fantastic experience to cook meals from our own produce. Therefore, it has been extremely difficult to choose food dishes for this book. I love them all! I might not have picked exactly the same courses as my grandmother would have chosen, but I am sure that she would have enjoyed these: Swedish meals with a modern twist.

Writing this cookbook has been like embarking on a food journey. I lived with it constantly for a short but intense time, during which I focused on little else. I got inspired as I tasted, tried, and loved the process that completely enveloped me. I have truly enjoyed every minute of this journey, and I hope that it will inspire you too. Enjoy, taste, and feel proud of our lovely Nordic kitchen!

Caroline Hofberg

Editor's note: Some of the more unique ingredients used in this recipe collection may not be available in your local grocery store. In many cases, a quick online search will yield plenty of options for purchasing those items. Ingredient amounts have been translated from the Swedish as accurately as possible, though in some cases they have been rounded up or down slightly for the convenience of the cook.

SMALL DISHES

Can you preserve traditional cuisine
and allow it to evolve naturally over time?

8–10 Pieces

Bottom
5 tbsp. butter
7 oz. dark rye bread

Filling
7 oz. cold-smoked salmon
1 small red onion
8.8 oz. cottage cheese
1 1/3 cups sour cream
3 tbsp. chopped dill
2 tbsp. freshly grated horseradish
salt
4 gelatin leaves

Garnish
cold-smoked salmon (thinly sliced)
lemon
dill

TART WITH SMOKED SALMON AND HORSERADISH

Birthday parties, baptisms, garden parties—oh my, what are we going to serve? One can only agree that sandwich tarts are a genius solution: delicious and easy to make and serve. This is a modern variation with smoked salmon and horseradish, thoroughly tested flavors that agree with most people. The tart is excellent on its own, as an appetizer, or as part of a buffet.

❦ Melt the butter and let it cool. Crumble the bread in a food processor. Add the butter and mix.

❦ Pour the crumb mixture into a springform pan or a cake pan with a removable bottom, about 9.5 inches in diameter.

❦ Use your hands to press the crumbs onto the bottom of the dish and a little bit around the edges. Store the dish in the fridge for at least an hour.

❦ Chop the salmon and the onion finely. Mix cottage cheese, sour cream, salmon, onion, dill, and horseradish. Add salt.

❦ Soak the gelatin leaves in cold water for about 5 minutes. Lift them out of the water and melt them on very low heat. Take 3 tablespoons of the salmon mix and add to the skillet with the gelatin. Pour the batter into the salmon mix and blend thoroughly.

❦ Spread the filling over the bottom. Cover with plastic wrap and let it cool and firm up in the fridge for at least 4 hours. Garnish with salmon roses, lemon, and dill before serving.

4 Portions

PANNA COTTA WITH CHIVES AND FISH ROE

2 gelatin leaves
1 cup cream
A few pinches freshly ground fennel seeds
1 cup plain yogurt
1/3 cup chopped chives
1/3 cup chopped dill
salt and freshly ground white pepper

Serve with
1.8 oz. fish roe
chopped red onion
chopped dill
a delicious rye bread

Serve panna cotta as an appetizer. Why not?

❋ Soak the gelatin leaves in cold water for 5 minutes.

❋ Simmer the cream and the fennel seeds until just boiling and remove from heat. Lift up the gelatin and stir into the cream.

❋ Blend yogurt and herbs into the cream and add salt and pepper.

❋ Pour the batter into four dishes, cups, or glasses. Place panna cotta in the fridge for at least 4 hours, until it is solid. Garnish with a click of roe, red onion, and dill. Serve with bread.

8–10 Pieces

OMELET TART WITH SMOKED MEAT

Omelet Batter
12 eggs
1 cup water
salt and freshly ground black pepper
butter for sautéing

Filling
14 oz. cream cheese (room temperature)
8.8 oz. cottage cheese
10 oz. smoked meat, i.e., reindeer
4 tbsp. freshly grated horseradish
salt
3.5 oz. baby spinach

This dish is "only" an omelet, but it never fails to impress. I usually make it for brunch or for the Easter table.

❋ *Omelets.* Lightly whisk the ingredients for the batter.

❋ Heat the butter in a frying pan, preferably Teflon. Pour a quarter of the batter into the pan and use a wooden spoon to stir until the batter firms up in the heat. Sauté the other three omelets the same way and let them cool off.

❋ *Filling.* Mix cream cheese and cottage cheese in a bowl. Cut the meat into tiny cubes. Mix the cheese blend, the meat, and the horseradish. And add salt.

❋ *The tart.* Place an omelet on a plate. Spread a layer of the filling over it and add some spinach. Place another omelet on top and repeat until you have all four omelets stacked with filling and spinach in between. Spread filling on top and decorate with a few spinach leaves.

Panna cotta with chives and fish roe, omelet tart with smoked meat

APPLE PANCAKE

I had to incorporate a pancake recipe. Skinny pancakes are a bit too time-consuming, but an oven pancake is more practical when the kids are trickling through the door. As a child, I used to request waffles with lingonberry cream whenever I visited my grandmother. It is still one of my favorites, and the yummy cream is a delicious addition to this pancake.

4 Portions

1 cup wheat flour
1/2 tsp. salt
2.5 cups milk
3 eggs
4 apples
2 tbsp. sugar
1 tsp. cinnamon
3 tbsp. hazelnuts (roughly chopped)

Serve with
1 cup whipped cream
3 tbsp. raw lingonberry jam

❋ Heat the oven at 425°F. Mix flour and salt in a deep bowl or pitcher.

❋ Add half of the milk and whisk until the batter is smooth. Add the rest of the milk. Finish off by whisking in the eggs, one by one.

❋ Core the apples and cut them into wedges. Mix them with sugar and cinnamon.

❋ Pour the batter into a roasting pan with parchment paper (or grease the pan). Press the apple wedges into the batter and sprinkle with the nuts.

❋ Bake the pancake in the middle of the oven until the batter is firm and has a nice color, about 25 minutes.

❋ Whip the cream and mix it with the lingonberry jam.

SPICED CHEESE PIE

6 Pieces

Pie Dough
1 1/3 cups sifted spelt flour
or wheat flour
1 stick butter
1 tbsp. cold water

Filling
3 eggs
1 cup light crème fraîche
scant 1/3 cup milk
salt and freshly ground white pepper
5–7 oz. seed-spiced cheese

An aged cheese belongs to the crawfish table. Personally, I love seed-spiced cheese and consider it an absolute must. I don't mind compromising, so instead I usually entertain with this pie with my favorite cheese in the filling. When the season allows it, this pie is delicious to garnish with butter-sautéed chanterelles.

⚜ Chop butter and flour into a crumbly mass. Add water and work into dough.

⚜ Press the dough into a tart pan with a removable bottom, about 10 inches in diameter. Prick the bottom with a fork and leave the piecrust in the fridge for at least 30 minutes.

⚜ Preheat the oven to 400°F. Bake the piecrust in the middle of the oven for 10 minutes.

⚜ Whisk eggs, crème fraîche, milk, salt, and pepper. Add the cheese. Pour the egg mix into the piecrust.

⚜ Bake the pie in the middle of the oven until it is thoroughly cooked and has a beautiful color, about 40 minutes. Let the pie "settle" before you cut it.

POTATO PIE WITH APPLE AND HERBS

6 Pieces

Piecrust
1 1/3 cups sifted spelt flour
or wheat flour
1 stick plus 1 tbsp. butter
1 tbsp. cold water

Filling
10 oz. boiled potatoes (cold)
1 cup diced apple
1 cup shredded leeks
5 tbsp. chopped dill
5 tbsp. chopped chives
3 eggs
1 cup light crème fraîche
1/3 cup milk
salt and freshly ground white pepper
1/2 cup grated cheese

This pie is excellent with smoked fish and cold cuts.

⚜ Chop butter and flour into a crumbly mass. Add water and work into dough.

⚜ Press the dough into a big pie dish, about 11 inches in diameter. Prick the bottom with a fork and leave the piecrust in the fridge for at least 30 minutes.

⚜ Preheat the oven to 400°F. Bake the piecrust in the middle of the oven for 10 minutes.

⚜ Slice the potatoes. Layer potatoes, apples, leeks, and herbs in the prebaked piecrust.

⚜ Whisk eggs, crème fraîche, milk, salt, and pepper. Pour the egg mix into the piecrust and sprinkle with the grated cheese.

⚜ Bake the pie in the middle of the oven until it is thoroughly baked and has a beautiful color, about 40 minutes.

POTATO SALAD WITH ASPARAGUS

4 Portions

approximately 2 lbs. fresh potatoes
17.5 oz. green asparagus
1 red onion (finely chopped)
3 tbsp. chopped dill
3 tbsp. roasted sunflower seeds

Dressing
1 tbsp. coarse-grain mustard
1 1/2 tbsp. fresh lemon juice
1 tbsp. water
1/3 cup cold-pressed rapeseed oil
salt and freshly ground white pepper

Here's a summer fresh potato salad that is delicious with smoked food, i.e., ham, turkey, or fish. If you want to vary this dish, you can exchange the asparagus for sugar peas. If you add crayfish tails or shrimp, this salad will transform into a main dish.

❋ *The dressing.* Whisk mustard, lemon juice, and water. Whisk in the oil, a little bit at a time. Finish off with salt and pepper.

❋ Boil the potatoes in lightly salted water. Let them cool off and then cut into smaller pieces. Pour the dressing over the potatoes.

❋ Cut off the coarse bottom part of the asparagus. Boil the asparagus in lightly salted water until it softens, about 4 minutes; it should still be slightly firm. Cut the asparagus into smaller pieces.

❋ Carefully blend potatoes, asparagus, onions, and dill. Serve the salad on a plate and sprinkle with sunflower seeds.

NEW POTATO SALAD WITH SALMON SAUCE

4 Portions

2 1/2 lbs. new potatoes
1 tbsp. salt
34 oz. water
1 tbsp. honey
1 red onion (finely chopped)
1/3 cup chopped dill
3 tbsp. chopped leek
3 tbsp. salmon sauce

Try this potato salad with smoked or gravlax fish. Delicious and summery!

❋ Scrub the potatoes until clean. Boil until soft in salted water with honey and a few dill stems.

❋ Mix the potatoes with leeks, onion, herbs, and salmon sauce.

Caesar salad of Norrland

Fall salad with lingon dressing

CAESAR SALAD OF NORRLAND

4 Portions

*5.3 oz. fresh mushrooms,
i.e., chanterelles
butter
salt and freshly ground white pepper
2 heads of iceberg lettuce
1 cup roughly grated Västerbotten cheese
or other aged cheese
about 5 oz. smoked reindeer roast
(thinly sliced)*

*Dressing
1 egg
2 anchovy fillets
fresh juice from 1/2 lemon
1 tbsp. coarse-grain mustard
1/2 tsp. Worcestershire sauce
2/3 cup cold-pressed rapeseed oil
2 tbsp. anchovy stock
salt and freshly ground white pepper*

*Croutons
3 round flatbreads, 5.5 inches in diameter
1 tbsp. cold-pressed rapeseed oil
1 pressed garlic clove
3/4 tsp. thyme*

This is an American classic that I have turned Swedish by adding mushrooms, smoked reindeer roast, aged cheese, and round flatbreads.

☘ *Croutons.* Preheat the oven to 325°F. Cut the bread into half-inch squares and put them into a bowl with oil, garlic, and thyme. Blend thoroughly.

☘ Spread the squares on a baking tray with parchment paper and roast them in the oven until they have a nice color, about 8 minutes. Let the croutons cool off.

☘ *Dressing.* Crack the egg into a food processor or into a bowl with a hand mixer. Add anchovies, lemon juice, mustard, and Worcestershire sauce. Mix until everything is blended. Blend oil and anchovy stock and add the oil drop by drop while mixing. Add salt and pepper.

☘ *Salad.* Clean the mushrooms and cut into smaller pieces. Sauté butter until the liquid is absorbed. Add salt and pepper.

☘ Break lettuce into pieces; don't cut with a knife because that makes it compact. Put the lettuce in ice-cold water so that it turns crisp. Let the water drip off thoroughly; it shouldn't be wet when mixed with the dressing.

☘ Mix the lettuce with mushrooms, cheese, and dressing right before you serve the salad. Blend so that all the lettuce leaves are covered in dressing. Arrange the meat on top of the salad and sprinkle with croutons.

FALL SALAD WITH LINGON DRESSING

4 Portions

*7 oz. beans, i.e., haricots verts
or wax beans
7 oz. fresh mushrooms, i.e., chanterelles
butter
2 tbsp. port wine
salt and freshly ground white pepper
2 1/2–3 1/2 cups loosely packed
lettuce leaves
about 2 oz. aged cheese*

*Lingon Dressing
1/3 cup lingonberries
1 tbsp. port wine
3 tbsp. cold-pressed rapeseed oil
1 tbsp. water
2 thyme leaves
salt and freshly ground white pepper*

This salad is the definition of fall. I usually serve it as an appetizer with a piece of bread or a nice piece of meat—perhaps wild.

☘ Blend the ingredients for the dressing.

☘ Parboil the beans in lightly salted water; they should still have a resistant consistency when chewed. Pour off the boiling water and rinse them in cold water.

☘ Clean the mushrooms and cut the bigger ones into smaller pieces. Sauté the mushrooms in butter until the liquid is absorbed. Add port wine and allow the liquid to absorb. Add salt and pepper.

☘ Serve the salad, beans, and mushrooms on plates and drizzle with dressing and finally sprinkle with cheese.

BEANS IN DILL PESTO

4 Portions

17.5 oz. beans, i.e., wax beans
or haricots verts

Dill Pesto
1/2 cup almonds
1 garlic clove
1 big bunch of dill
1/2 cup grated Prästost
or other aged cheese
1/2 cup cold-pressed rapeseed oil
salt and freshly ground black pepper

Okay, I know. Pesto is not very Swedish. But make it with dill, aged cheese, and a nice cold-pressed rape-seed oil, and you have a Nordic pesto. Throw in some beans and it will turn out prettier, healthier, and yummier. Not a bad combination. Good for the buffet, or in combination with most dishes, i.e., with grilled or warm-smoked salmon.

❧ Begin with the pesto: Mix almonds, garlic, and dill. Add the cheese and finally the oil. Add salt and pepper.

❧ Parboil the beans for a few minutes in lightly salted water; they should still have some resistance when chewed. Pour out the boiling water and let the beans drain thoroughly.

❧ Mix beans and pesto and marinate for at least 1 hour so that the flavors mature.

BEET SALAD WITH PORK AND BLUE CHEESE

4 Portions

about 28 oz. beets
about 7 oz. salted bacon
1.8 oz. walnuts
about 3 cups of endives
5 oz. blue cheese

Dressing
1 1/2 tbsp. fresh lemon juice
3 tbsp. cold-pressed rapeseed oil
salt and freshly ground black pepper

The beets' natural sweetness is brought out with a bit of saltiness. Crispy bacon and blue cheese are nice flavor companions to the red knobs.

❧ Boil the beets until soft in lightly salted water; time varies depending on the size of the beets, between 15 minutes and 1 hour. Keep some of the tops and the root while you boil them; it will preserve the color and the taste.

❧ Shred the bacon and sauté until crisp and then let it dry off on paper towels. Roast the walnuts in a dry, hot pan and break them into smaller pieces.

❧ Mix the ingredients for the dressing.

❧ Briefly rinse the beets under cold water and press the peel away while they are still warm.

❧ Cut the beets into wedges and mix in the dressing.

❧ Serve salad, beets, and bacon. Crumble the cheese on top and then the walnuts.

ALMOND POTATO SOUP WITH ANCHOVIES

4 Portions

about 21 oz. almond potatoes
1 big leek
34 oz. chicken or vegetable bouillon
1 1/2 tsp. thyme
1 cup milk
salt and freshly ground white pepper

Topping
2 yellow onions
butter
6 anchovy fillets
2 tsp. anchovy stock
1 tbsp. thyme
preferably lemon thyme

In the beginning of the history of the Swedish potato, it was mostly used to make vodka. It wasn't until home distilling was forbidden in the middle of the 1800s that it was understood that potatoes were an excellent food source.

♣ Peel the potatoes and cut into smaller pieces. Rinse and shred the leek.

♣ Boil the potatoes, the leek, the bouillon, and the thyme. Cover the pot and boil until the potatoes are soft, about 15 minutes.

♣ Whisk or mix the soup until it is thick and turbid, preferably with a few pieces of potatoes left.

♣ Add milk and simmer the soup for a few more minutes. Add pepper and salt to your taste, but remember that the anchovies are salty.

♣ *Topping.* Peel and cut the onion into skinny wedges. Sauté it slowly in butter until it is soft, about 10–15 minutes. Chop the anchovies and add to the mix with the stock and thyme and let everything melt together.

MINESTRONE WITH GAME STOCK

4 Portions

8.5 oz. game stock
1 yellow onion
1 large carrot
1 piece of celeriac, about 3.5 oz.
2 potatoes
1 leek
3.5 oz. haricot verts
butter
6 1/2 cups water
3 tbsp. game stock with chanterelles
1 tsp. thyme
2 tbsp. tomato puree
salt and freshly ground black pepper
1/3 cup chopped parsley
about 1.8 oz. Västerbotten cheese or any well-aged cheese

A meat soup made my way, with a taste of the wild.

♣ Peel and chop the onion. Peel the carrot, the celery, and the potatoes and cut into small cubes. Rinse and shred the leek and halve the beans.

♣ Fry the onion, carrot, and celery in butter in a pot, just until translucent. Add the meat and brown it while shredding it with a fork.

♣ Add water, stock, thyme, and tomato puree. Cover with a lid and boil the soup for about 10 minutes.

♣ Mix potatoes, leeks, and beans. Keep boiling until all the vegetables are soft, about 10 minutes. Add salt and pepper and mix in the parsley.

♣ Serve the soup with sliced or roughly grated cheese.

CHANTARELLE ROLL WITH VÄSTERBOTTEN CHEESE

6–8 Portions

Dough
4 tbsp. butter
1/3 cup wheat flour
2 cups milk
3 egg yolks
1 tsp. baking powder
3 egg whites

Filling
2 yellow onions
10 oz. chanterelles
butter
2/3 cup chopped parsley
1 cup grated well-aged cheese, i.e.,
Västerbotten cheese
salt and freshly ground black pepper

For Baking
2/3 cup grated well-aged cheese, i.e.,
Västerbotten cheese

Perfect as a late-night snack, or on the buffet or perhaps as a filling and flavorful surprise at the crayfish party; this dish is suitable for many occasions.

❧ Heat the oven to 475°F. Melt the butter. Whisk the flour and dilute it with milk. Boil on low heat while stirring, about 5 minutes. Move the skillet from the heat.

❧ Stir down the egg yolks, one at a time, and add the baking powder. In a separate bowl, whisk the egg whites until they stiffen and carefully turn them into the batter.

❧ Pour the batter into a roasting pan with parchment paper. Bake in the middle of the oven for about 10 minutes.

❧ Meanwhile, make the filling: Chop the onion and the mushrooms. Fry the onion in butter but without browning it. Add the mushrooms and sauté until the liquid has evaporated. Add the parsley, cheese, salt, and pepper.

❧ Spread the filling over the bottom. Roll the whole thing up and set with the edge facing down. You can prepare this dish up to this point ahead of time.

❧ Sprinkle with grated cheese and bake in the middle of the oven until the roll has acquired a nice color, about 10 minutes.

❧ Serve it warm or lukewarm.

MUSHROOM RISOTTO WITH CELERY AND APPLE

4 Portions

1 yellow onion
1 piece of celeriac, 7 tbsp. butter
for sautéing
1 3/4 cups arborio rice
3 tbsp. game stock with chanterelle
1 cup dry white wine
about 5 cups boiling hot water
7 oz. fresh mushrooms, i.e., chanterelles
or funnel chanterelles
salt and freshly ground black pepper
1 red apple
1 1/3 cups roughly grated aged cheese,
i.e., Västerbotten cheese

In the fall the forest offers an abundance of flavorful ingredients. The Swedish kitchen thrives on its rich woods. Fill your kitchen with the smells of the forest while you make this deliciously creamy risotto with mushrooms, celeriac, and apple.

❧ Peel and chop onion and celery. Fry in butter in a pot without browning the vegetables.

❧ Stir in the rice and sauté for a little bit until the grains turn glossy. Add the stock and wine and let it boil until absorbed.

❧ Pour hot water over the rice until it is covered and boil until the liquid is absorbed. Continue to cook the risotto like this. Dilute with a little bit of water and allow it to boil until absorbed before you add more liquid. Stir continuously. Boil the rice until it is evenly soft and creamy, about 20 minutes.

❧ Sauté the mushrooms in butter until all the liquid is absorbed and add salt and pepper. Rinse the apple and cut it into small pieces.

❧ Stir the mushrooms, the apple pieces, and the cheese into the risotto. Cover with a lid and let it sit for 3–5 minutes. Add salt and pepper and taste. Add more water if you need to. The risotto should be creamy.

ROOT VEGETABLE SALAD WITH HERB VINAIGRETTE

4 Portions

14 oz. potatoes
10 oz. carrots
7 oz. turnip
7 oz. parsnip
34 oz. water and 2 cubes
of vegetable bouillon
1/2 tsp. salt

Dressing
1/2 cup chopped dill
1/2 cup chopped chives
1 chopped garlic clove
1/4 cup bouillon from the
root vegetable boil
2 tsp. vinegar essence, 12 percent
1/3 cup cold-pressed rapeseed oil
salt and freshly ground white pepper

You can enrich the classic potato salad with typical Swedish root vegetables. This salad is tasty with anything that you would normally eat with potato salad. Cold cuts, smoked fish, and tjälknöl (English translation: "frost bump," frozen cooked meat). This variation is delicious whether you eat it warm, lukewarm, or cold.

🌿 Peel and cut potatoes and root vegetables into smaller pieces.

🌿 Boil water, bouillon, and salt. Boil the root vegetables for 5 minutes.

🌿 Add the potatoes and continue to boil for about 8 minutes. The potatoes and root vegetables should be soft but not mushy. Pour out the bouillon, but save 1/4 cup for the dressing.

🌿 *The dressing.* Mix herbs, garlic, bouillon, and vinegar essence. Add the oil drop by drop. Taste and add pepper and salt to your liking.

🌿 Mix the root vegetables in the dressing.

ROOT VEGETABLE SALAD WITH SPELT

4 Portions

1 cup whole spelt grains
1 3/4 cups water and 1 vegetable
bouillon cube
2. 1/4 lbs root vegetables, i.e., carrots,
beets, parsnip, celeriac
2 red onions
2 tbsp. cold-pressed rapeseed oil

Dressing
1 tbsp. cold-pressed rapeseed oil
1 tbsp. freshly squeezed lemon juice
1 tbsp. liquid honey
1 tsp. ground ginger
1/2 cup chopped leaf parsley
salt and freshly ground white pepper

Cheese Medley
5.3 oz. aged cheese,
i.e., Prästost (priest cheese)
or schnapps cheese
8.8 oz. cottage cheese

Spelt is an ancient grain that has not been refined, and it has been cultivated in many cultures for thousands of years. Spelt is very nutritious, and you can buy it as whole grain, bran, sifted flour, or wholemeal flour. Here, I have chosen to use the whole grains in the root vegetable salad. A cheese medley complements this yummy vegetarian dinner dish.

🌿 Boil the spelt grain in the bouillon covered, until soft, about 40 minutes. Pour out the excessive boil water.

🌿 Mix the ingredients for the dressing.

🌿 Heat the oven to 425°F. Peel the root vegetables and cut them into smaller pieces. Peel and cut the onions into thick wedges. Put the root vegetables and the onion on a baking tray covered with parchment paper. Drizzle with oil. Roast in the middle of the oven for about 25 minutes.

🌿 Mix the root vegetable with the spelt and dressing. Add salt and pepper.

🌿 *Cheese medley.* Grate cheese on the fine side of the grater and mix with cottage cheese.

DILL BLINIS WITH ROE CRÈME

15 Big or 30 Small

2 eggs
2 cups milk, 2 percent
1 oz. yeast
1 cup wheat flour
3/4 cup buckwheat flour
1 tsp. salt
1/2 cup finely chopped dill
4 tbsp. butter

Serve with
roe crème
red onion
dill
lemon

Transform fluffy Russian minipancakes into an elegant appetizer with classic Swedish flavor favorites: dill and fish roe.

🍃 Separate egg whites and yolks.

🍃 Heat the milk until lukewarm, 98.6°F. Pour some of the milk into a cup and mix the yeast into it.

🍃 Whisk the flour into the rest of the milk. Add the yeast mix, egg yolks, salt, and dill. Whisk until the batter is even. Cover with a plate and let it ferment for 1 hour in room temperature.

🍃 Melt the butter and let it cool off. Whisk the egg whites until they stiffen into firm foam. Mix the batter with the butter and turn down the egg whites right before cooking.

🍃 Cook the pancakes slowly on a griddle or blin pan. Use about 1 1/2 tbsp. of batter for each blin on a griddle, or about 1 cup of batter for a blin pan. Turn the minipancakes when they begin to set and dry and bubbles form on the surface.

🍃 Place the blin on a plate. You can also keep them warm in the oven for about 5 minutes at 325°F. Serve with roe crème and garnish with chopped red onion, dill, and lemon wedges.

ROE CRÈME

6 Portions

1 cup crème fraîche
3.5 oz. fish roe
2 tbsp. finely chopped red onion
1 ml grated lemon peel
salt and freshly ground white pepper

🍃 Use an electric whisk to beat crème fraîche until it stiffens, about 2–3 minutes. Carefully add roe, onion, and lemon peel.

🍃 Season with salt and pepper to your liking.

ROOT VEGETABLE JANSSON

4 portions

2 yellow onions
butter for sautéing
4 potatoes (starchy kind,
i.e., King Edward)
10 oz. turnip
2 carrots
1 can anchovy fillets, 4.4 oz.
1 1/3 cups cream, or use half cream and
half milk
2 tbsp. bread crumbs
2 tbsp. butter

An honorable Jansson by all means, but I like to mix in some root vegetables to add more flavor.

🌿 Preheat the oven at 400°F. Peel the onions and cut into thin slices. Sauté it soft in butter.

🌿 Peel potatoes, parsnip, and carrots and cut into thin "Jansson strips."

🌿 Layer potatoes, root vegetables, onions, and anchovies in a baking dish.

🌿 Pour a few drops of the anchovy liquid on top before you cover with cream. Sprinkle the bread crumbs over and add pats of butter on top.

🌿 Bake in the middle of the oven until the potatoes and the root vegetables are soft and the gratin has a nice color, about 45 minutes.

ANCHOVY TART

8–10 Pieces

Bottom
5 tbsp. butter
7 oz. dark rye bread

Filling
1 jar anchovies fillets, 4.4 oz.
1 yellow onion
1 1/3 cups sour cream
8.8 oz. cottage cheese
2 tbsp. liquid from the anchovies
freshly ground white pepper
4 gelatin leaves

Garnish
chopped chives

This salty tart with anchovies is delicious and looks beautiful on the herring table.

🌿 Melt the butter and let it cool off. Pulse the bread in a food processor until it turns to crumbs. Add the butter and mix.

🌿 Transfer the crumb mix into a tart pan with a removable bottom, about 9.5 inches in diameter. Press the crumbs over the bottom of the dish and a little bit around the edges. Put the dish into the fridge for at least 1 hour.

🌿 Drain the anchovies, but save the liquid. Chop the anchovy fillets. Peel and chop the onions finely.

🌿 Mix anchovies, onion, sour cream, cottage cheese, and the liquid from the anchovies.

🌿 Soak the gelatin leaves in cold water for about 5 minutes. Lift them out of the water and melt them on low heat. Add 3 tbsp. of the anchovy mix into the pan and stir it with the gelatin. Pour the gelatin batter into the anchovy mix and mix thoroughly.

🌿 Pour the filling over the bottom. Cover with plastic foil and let the tart chill in the fridge for at least 4 hours. Sprinkle generously with chopped chives right before serving the tart.

CAPTAIN MEDLEY

About 1 3/4 Cups

2 bucklings
1 hard-boiled egg
1/2 red onion
1 bunch chives
1/4 cup mayo
1/2 cup sour cream
1 tbsp. capers
freshly ground white pepper

🍃 Clean the buckling meticulously so that all the bones are gone. Peel and chop the egg, onion, and chives.

🍃 Mix all the ingredients. Allow the flavors to settle for at least 1 hour in the fridge.

CRAYFISH MEDLEY WITH ROE

About 1 3/4 Cups

1 jar crayfish tails (about 13 oz.)
1 stem celery
1/2 cup mayo
2/3 cup crème fraîche
2 tbsp. fish roe
3 tbsp. chopped chives
salt and freshly ground white pepper

🍃 Let the liquid drip off the crayfish tails and chop them roughly. Chop celery finely.

🍃 Mix all the ingredients. Allow the flavors to settle for at least 1 hour in the fridge.

GRAVLAX MEDLEY

About 2 Cups

7 oz. gravlax
1 1/3 cups light crème fraîche
4 tbsp. light mayo
2 tbsp. grated horseradish
4 tbsp. chopped chives
1/2 tsp. freshly ground white pepper

🍃 Cut the salmon into small pieces.

🍃 Mix all the ingredients. Allow the flavors to settle for at least 1 hour in the fridge.

OLD MAN'S MEDLEY

About 1 3/4 Cups

4 hard-boiled eggs
1 small yellow onion
1 small jar of anchovy fillets, 2 oz.
1 raw egg yolk
1/4 cup chopped dill
1.8 oz. salmon roe or other large-beaded caviar

🍃 Peel and chop the eggs. Chop onion and anchovies finely.

🍃 Mix all the ingredients and add the caviar last. Allow the flavors to settle for at least 1 hour in the fridge.

Different medleys with herring, smoked fish, and fish roe are a nice addition to the herring table during midsummer as well as at Christmastime. Or perhaps as an appetizer: a salty medley on crisp bread or rye bread. They also stimulate the taste buds at the summer picnic or when you are craving a night snack.

JANSSON'S MEDLEY *About 1 3/4 Cups*

About 10 oz. cooked cold potatoes	*4 tbsp. chopped chives*
1/2 yellow onion	*1 1/3 cups sour cream*
1 small jar anchovy fillets, 2 oz.	*salt*
2 tsp. liquid from the anchovies	*freshly ground white pepper*

❧ Peel and cube the potatoes. Chop onion and anchovies finely.

❧ Mix all the ingredients. Allow the flavors to settle for at least 1 hour in the fridge.

BUCKLING MEDLEY *About 1 3/4 Cups*

6 bucklings	*2 tbsp. chopped capers*
1 cup sour cream	*salt and freshly ground white pepper*
4 tbsp. relish	*1/4 cup chopped dill*

❧ Clean the buckling thoroughly so that all the bones are removed. Chop it coarsely.

❧ Mix all the ingredients. Allow the flavors to settle for at least 1 hour in the fridge. Garnish with sliced radishes and chopped chives.

KALLES KAVIAR DIP *About 1 1/3 Cups*

4.4 oz. cottage cheese	*3 tbsp. finely chopped leek*
3.5 oz. cream cheese	*freshly ground white pepper*
1/2 cup lightly smoked caviar, i.e., Kalles	

❧ Mix all the ingredients. Allow the flavors to settle for at least 1 hour in the fridge.

ROE MEDLEY WITH A DASH OF GIN

About 1 3/4 Cups

3.5 oz. cream cheese	*3.5 oz. roe*
1/2 cup sour cream	*1 1/2 tbsp. gin*
4 tbsp. finely chopped red onion	*freshly ground white pepper*
4 tbsp. chopped dill	

❧ Mix all the ingredients. Allow the flavors to settle for at least 1 hour in the fridge.

SANDWICH WITH BUCKLING

4–6 Pieces

2 bucklings
4 slices coarse rye bread
butter
lettuce
radishes
chives

Ship Medley
1/4 cup chopped sour pickled gherkin
1/4 cup chopped chives
1/2 cup cottage cheese
2 1/2 tbsp. lightly smoked caviar,
i.e., Kalles
2 hard-boiled eggs
salt and freshly ground white pepper

Super Swedish sandwich that is excellent on a sunny summer day as well as toward the small hours of the night.

❦ *Ship medley.* Mix gherkins, chives, cottage cheese, and caviar. Chop the eggs and blend into the mix. Add salt and pepper.

❦ Thoroughly clean the buckling and cut into coarse pieces.

❦ Spread a thin layer of butter on the bread and add a little bit of salad. Add a click of the ship medley and put the buckling, sliced radishes, and chopped chives on top.

MARINATED BALTIC HERRING ON CRISP BREAD

4–6 Portions

21 oz. Baltic herring fillets
1 tsp. salt
1 ml pepper
1/2 cup coarse rye or spelt flour
butter for sautéing

Marinade
1 egg
1 cup milk, 2 percent
1 1/2 tbsp. chopped capers
3 tbsp. coarse-grained mustard
1 tbsp. grated yellow onion
1/3 cup chopped dill

Serve with
quark with horseradish
crisp bread
red onion rings
capers

Sautéed herring on crisp bread—it can barely get tastier than that.

❦ Rinse the herring, let it drip off, and pat it dry with paper towels.

❦ Whisk the ingredients for the marinade in a bowl. Add the herring and let it marinade in the fridge for 4–6 hours.

❦ Take out the herring and let it drip in a colander. Combine flour, salt, and pepper. Fold the fillets double and turn them in the flour mixture. Sauté the herring in butter until golden brown.

❦ Spread quark on the crisp bread and add the sautéed herring. Garnish with onion rings and capers.

BUCKLING BOX WITH HORSERADISH

4 Portions

10 oz. cleaned buckling fillet
1 small leek
1/2 cup chopped dill
1/2 cup cream with 27 percent
fat content
2–3 tbsp. grated horseradish
salt

This delicious buckling box is an excellent fit on the herring table as well as the midsummer buffet, but it is also a simple and practical summer dish that pairs nicely with new potatoes.

❧ Preheat the oven to 425°F. Make sure that the buckling fillet does not contain any bones. Rinse and shred the leek.

❧ Put the buckling in a baking dish. Spread leek and dill over the fish.

❧ Mix cream, horseradish, and salt and pour over the fillets. Bake in the middle of the oven for about 20 minutes.

STRIPED BUCKLING BOX

4 Portions

4 large bucklings
2 tbsp. coarse-grained mustard
2 tbsp. light mayo
1 cup light crème fraîche
salt
2 hard-boiled eggs (chopped)
1/2 cup chopped pickles
1/2 cup chopped pickled beets
1 finely chopped red onion
chopped chives

If this doesn't taste delicious in the summer out in the archipelago, then I don't know what does. Perfect for lunch with potatoes, crisp bread, and a glass of cold beer. Or why not inlcude it as part of a buffet? You can make the buckling box way ahead of time, but wait to add the beets because they have a tendency to color the rest of the dish.

❧ Clean the buckling thoroughly so that all the bones are gone. Put the pieces on a plate.

❧ Mix mustard, mayo, and crème fraîche. Add salt.

❧ Spread the mustard sauce over the buckling.

❧ Stripe the buckling with egg, cucumbers, beets, and red onion. Garnish with chives.

CAVIAR AND POTATO BOX

4 Portions

17–21 oz. potatoes (floury kind, i.e., King Edward)
1 yellow onion
1/2 cup lightly smoked caviar, i.e., Kalles
1 1/3 cups milk, 2 percent
3 eggs
1/3 cup chopped dill
freshly ground white pepper

You don't need to go abroad for long to start longing for Kalles caviar. This potato box is always one of the first things I make after coming home from a trip.

🌿 Preheat the oven to 400°F. Peel and cut the potatoes and onion. Layer potatoes and onion in a buttered baking pan.

🌿 Whisk caviar, milk, eggs, dill, and pepper. Pour the egg mix into the dish.

🌿 Bake in the middle of the oven until the potatoes are soft and the box has a nice color, about 30–40 minutes.

HERRING BOX WITH ROE SAUCE

4 Portions

21 oz. Baltic herring fillet
1 tsp. salt
1 3/4 cups shredded leek
4 tbsp. chopped dill
lemon peel and juice from 1/2 lemon
1/2 cup cream with 27 percent fat content, or whipping cream
3 tbsp. chopped chives
3.5 oz. roe

Baltic herring is inexpensive, but here it is served with roe for added luxury.

🌿 Preheat the oven to 425°F. Rinse the herring and allow it to drain thoroughly. Salt the fleshy side and fold the fillets across. Put them in a baking dish.

🌿 Spread leek, dill, lemon peel, and juice over the herring.

🌿 Bake the box in the middle of the oven for about 20 minutes.

🌿 Beat the cream. Add chives and fish roe. Put a click of the cream on top of the warm herring and allow it to melt.

LEMON AND ONION HERRING

4–6 Portions

1 jar pickled herring	*peel from 1/2 lemon*
15 oz. pickles, thinly cut into strips	*1/2 cup water*
1 small red onion, thinly sliced	*1 cup sugar*
3 tbsp. vinegar essence, 12 percent	*6 allspice berries*
4 inches of leek, shredded	*6 cloves*
juice from 1/2 lemon	*2 bay leaves*

❧ Boil the ingredients for the pickle and let it cool off.

❧ Rinse the herring fillets in cold water and allow the liquid to drip off. Cut the fillets into smaller pieces.

❧ Layer the ingredients in a thoroughly cleaned jar. Pour in the cold pickling mixture. Store the herring in a cool place for at least 24 hours before you serve it.

JUNIPER BERRY HERRING

4–6 Portions

1 jar pickled herring	*1/2 cup water*
15 oz. pickles	*4 inches leek, cut into thin strips*
1 carrot, thinly sliced	*1 cup sugar*
3 tbsp. vinegar essence, 12 percent	*10 crushed juniper berries*
1 small red onion, thinly sliced	*3 tbsp. gin*

❧ Boil the ingredients for the pickle and let it cool off.

❧ Rinse the herring fillets in cold water and allow them to drip off. Cut them into smaller pieces.

❧ Layer the ingredients in a thoroughly cleaned jar. Pour the pickling mixture inside. Store the herring in a cool place for at least 24 hours before serving it.

AQUAVIT HERRING WITH ROOT VEGETABLES

4–6 Portions

1 jar pickled herring	*4 inches leek, shredded*
15 oz. pickle	*1 cup sugar*
1 carrot, thinly sliced	*1 red apple, cut into cubes*
3 tbsp. vinegar essence, 12 percent	*3 tbsp. aquavit*
1.8 oz. celery root (thinly shredded)	*1 tsp. whole caraway*
2/3 cup water	*1 tsp. whole fennel seeds*

❧ Boil the ingredients for the pickle and let it cool.

❧ Rinse the herring fillets in cold water and allow the liquid to drip off. Cut the fillets into smaller pieces.

❧ Layer the ingredients in a thoroughly cleaned jar. Pour the cold pickle into the jar. Store the herring in a cool place for at least 24 hours before you serve it.

CAVIAR GRAVLAX HERRING

4–6 Portions

21 oz. Baltic herring fillet sauce	*1/3 cup vinegar essence, 12 percent*
1/3 cup sour cream	*3 tbsp. lightly smoked caviar, i.e., Kalles*
pickle	*1 tbsp. salt*
1/3 cup mayo	*1/2 finely chopped red onion*
2 cups water	*1/3 cup chopped dill*
2 tbsp. coarse-grained mustard	*freshly ground white pepper*

❧ Rinse the herring. Mix the ingredients for the pickle. Let the fillets soak in it until the meat turns white, 4–6 hours.

❧ Take out the fillets and allow the liquid to drip off thoroughly, preferably by first using a colander, and then put the fillets on a thick layer of paper towels that will soak up any superfluous liquid; otherwise, the sauce will be diluted. Pull off the skin when the fillets are thoroughly dried off.

❧ Mix the ingredients for the sauce. Carefully put down the herring in it. Store in the fridge for at least 24 hours before you serve it.

There are endless variations on herring recipes. Today you can buy soaked, salty herring fillets in a jar, so the process is even easier. Just let your imagination flow and create your own favorites. It is always good to begin with lots of onions, preferably in different colors.

HERRING SALAD

An old favorite, here in a simple and creamier variation.

2 jars sweet-pickled herring, each 7 oz.
1/2 apple
1/2 cup finely cubed pickled beets
1 cup light crème fraîche
4 tbsp. chopped yellow onion
3 tbsp. chopped sour pickled gherkins
chopped chives

🍃 Strain the herring from liquid. Cut the herring and apple into small pieces.

🍃 Mix herring, apple, beets, crème fraîche, onion, and gherkin.

🍃 Allow the flavors to mature in the fridge for at least 1 hour. Garnish with chopped chives.

SCHNAPPS SALAD

You can never go wrong with this popular salty medley with sweet-pickled herring and caviar.

10 oz. cooked cold newly harvested potatoes
1 jar sweet-pickled herring, 7 oz.
1/2 cup sour cream
2/3 cup mayo
2 tbsp. lightly smoked caviar, i.e., Kalles
1/3 cup chopped leek
4 tbsp. chopped red onion
1 bunch chopped dill
freshly ground white pepper

🍃 Cut the potatoes into cubes and the herring into small pieces.

🍃 Mix sour cream, mayo, caviar, onion, and dill. And add some pepper.

🍃 Mix sauce, potatoes, and herring. Allow the flavors to mature in the fridge for at least 1 hour.

SWEET-PICKLED SALAD WITH APPLE SAUCE

This is a fresher alternative to the old and honorable sweet-pickled herring with sour cream. It is excellent for lunch when the summer guests arrive at the country house.

4 sweet-pickled herring fillets
4–6 cooked cold potatoes
2 hard-boiled eggs
2 tomatoes
1 bunch of scallions or a piece of leek
lettuce

Dressing
1 finely cubed apple
1/3 cup finely cubed sour pickled gherkin
1 1/3 cups sour cream
1 tbsp. coarse-grained mustard
salt and freshly ground white pepper

🍃 Begin by mixing the ingredients for the dressing.

🍃 Cut the herring and potatoes into smaller pieces and eggs and tomatoes into wedges. Rinse and cut the leek into strips. Break the lettuce into smaller pieces.

🍃 Put the lettuce, potatoes, tomatoes, and herring on a plate. Put the egg wedges on top and spread leeks on top.

🍃 Drizzle a little bit of dressing on top and serve the rest of it on the side.

You can easily make your own beautiful ice bowls for small schnapps bottles. Select two bowls or pans that can be stacked inside each other. Remember that there has to be a little bit of space in between the bowls. Fill the space with water and tape the bowls crosswise to keep the bowls in place. You can also place something heavy in the top bowl to keep it down. Stick flowers or herbs into the space with the water and put the bowls in the freezer for at least 24 hours before you use the ice bowl that will have formed in between the two bowls. Place the ice bowl on a plate and decorate with a little bit of greenery and put little schnapps bottles inside.

You can also use an empty milk carton, a little pail, or something similar. Decorate with beautiful flowers all around and fill with water. Put in the freezer overnight and remove the carton and serve.

TASTY TIPS

It is a lot of fun to treat guests to home-spiced schnapps. Use what nature has to offer or search your spice pantry for interesting flavors. It is best to use vodka that has a fairly low alcohol content as it will bring out the best aroma in the spices and berries. Usually it is enough to soak the spices for a few hours, but if you want schnapps with a bit more zing, you should allow them to soak for 24 hours. The rule of thumb is that the more potent the spice, the less time is needed. If you want to create an essence, leave the spices in the alcohol for a week. Use a jar with a lid and shake it every day. After a week you will have a powerful essence that you can dilute to desired strength. Sugar—sugar cube, a spoon of raw sugar, or a little bit of honey—will accentuate the flavor and aroma.

JUNIPER BERRIES

Put crushed juniper berries and possibly a little bit of shredded lemon peel in the vodka. Let it stand for at least 24 hours, strain, and dilute until the drink has your desired strength. This is tasty with smoked salted leg of mutton, wild meat, and smoked fish.

ALLSPICE

Allow the allspice to settle in the vodka for at least 24 hours. Strain and dilute until you achieve desired strength. This is tasty with pickled and spiced herring and *lutfisk* (traditional Nordic dish: stockfish in lye).

BITTER ORANGE AND RAISIN

Let dried pieces of bitter orange and raisins soak in vodka for a few hours, possibly with a little bit of raw sugar. Strain and taste. This is tasty with Christmas ham and spareribs.

EVERGREEN SPROUTS

Preferably use delicate evergreen sprouts and allow them to soak in the vodka for 24 hours. Sweeten with a little bit of honey and possibly add a little bit of gin. This is tasty with midsummer's herring buffet, the Christmas table, wild meat, and smoked fish.

CLOVE

Soak whole cloves in vodka for a few hours and strain. If necessary, dilute the drink until you achieve desired strength. This is tasty with Christmas herring, ham, and spareribs.

LINGONBERRIES

Soak lingonberries in vodka, at least overnight. Sweeten with a little bit of raw sugar or honey and add a bit of gin if you so desire. Taste and strain to remove the berries. This is tasty with meatballs, dried salted leg of mutton, spareribs, and wild meat.

GLOGG SPICE

Let a bag of glogg spices soak in vodka for a few hours with a little bit of raw sugar. Strain away the spices and taste. If you wish, dilute until you achieve the desired strength. This is tasty with the Christmas table or serve with coffee to digest all the holiday food.

BLUEBERRY AND CINNAMON

Soak blueberries and cinnamon sticks in the schnapps overnight. Sweeten with a little bit of honey. Taste and strain the drink. This is tasty with meatballs, spareribs, and ham.

WELCOME TO THE COCKTAIL PARTY!

Once upon a time, the cocktail party was an event that lasted for a limited time, just until dinner was served. Today, it has developed into a party that often lasts all night long, accompanied by delicious drinks and savory snacks. Here are some special drinks for special moments. You will find appetizing nibbles on page 58.

1 Glass

1.35 oz. gin
0.7 oz. lingonberry concentrate
0.33 oz. dry vermouth
ice
frozen lingonberries

LINGON DRY MARTINI

♣ Chill the glasses with ice or place them in the freezer for a while.

♣ Mix gin, lingonberry concentrate, vermouth, and ice. Sift into a glass and add a few frozen lingonberries.

1 Glass

0.7–1 oz. cloudberry
or blackberry liqueur
about 7 oz. dry sparkling wine
or champagne
a few frozen cloudberries or blackberries

KIR SUEDOISE

♣ Pour the liqueur into a champagne glass.

♣ Fill with sparkling wine and add frozen berries.

1 Glass

0.7 oz. cloudberry liqueur
1.35 oz. vodka
ice
frozen cloudberries or blackberries

NORDIC APERITIF

♣ Chill the glasses with a little bit of ice or keep them in the freezer for a little bit.

♣ Mix the liqueur with vodka and ice. Pour into a glass and add frozen berries.

1 Glass

0.5 oz. gin
0.5 oz. concentrated elderflower juice
about 7 oz. dry sparkling wine
or champagne

SPARKLING GIN AND ELDER

♣ Pour gin and juice into a champagne glass.

♣ Add the wine.

APPETIZERS

These appetizers with their Nordic flavors will taste even better with the cocktails on page 57. You can prepare these snacks ahead of time, because nobody wants to be stuck in the kitchen when the guests arrive.

FALL CROUSTADES

24 Pieces

1 box mini croustades (24 pieces)
chives

Filling

1 shallot	2/3 cup whipping cream
1 clove of garlic	1/2 apple
3 tbsp. dry sherry	salt and freshly ground white pepper
3.5 oz. fresh mushrooms	3 tbsp. finely chopped celery root

❧ Chop onion, garlic, mushrooms, and apple finely. Sauté onion, garlic, mushrooms, and celery root in a little butter until the veggies are soft but not brown.

❧ Add sherry and cream. Boil on low heat until most of the liquid has absorbed. Add salt and pepper. You can prepare this beforehand.

❧ Heat the oven to 400°F. Heat the croustades for a few minutes right before you serve these snacks. Fill the croustades with warm filling and garnish with chopped chives. Serve them immediately while they are still crispy.

MUTTON TAPAS

About 20 Pieces

3.5–5.3 oz. smoked dried salted leg of mutton or reindeer roast, thinly sliced
4.4 oz. quark cheese with horseradish

❧ Overlap the meat slices so that you form a rectangle, about 10 × 13 inches, on plastic wrap.

❧ Spread cheese (room temperature) on top and roll the slices into a log. Tightly wrap the plastic around the meat log.

❧ Store in the fridge for at least a few hours and cut into slices before serving.

TOAST WITH GREEN SHRIMP CRÈME

16 Pieces

	Serve with
1 cup green peas	
about 2 tbsp. mayo	16 round slices of pumpernickel
7 oz. peeled shrimp	bread
salt	lemon

❧ Parboil the peas for about 4 minutes. Strain them but save some of the water. Mix the peas with 1 tbsp. of the water until you have a smooth puree.

❧ Mix the puree with mayo, adding a little bit at a time. The mayo should just bind the mixture into a creamy puree. Mix in roughly chopped shrimp and add salt and Tabasco. Spread the shrimp crème on the bread rounds and garnish with lemon and dill.

TOAST NORDIC

16 Pieces

	Serve with
3.5 oz. smoked reindeer roast (thinly sliced)	
1/2 cup cottage cheese	3.5 oz. fish roe
3 tbsp. mayo	16 small round slices of
1 tsp. coarse-grained mustard	dark rye bread
3 tbsp. chopped chives	chives
salt and freshly ground white pepper	

❧ Chop meat into small pieces. Mix meat, cottage cheese, mayo, mustard, chives, salt, and pepper.

❧ Strain the fish roe through a colander so that it gets firmer and easier to use as garnish.

❧ Distribute the reindeer medley on the bread and garnish with fish roe and chives.

HEATING POWER TEARS

Perfect after the skiing trip, the winter walk, or perhaps the last cleaning day of the fall in the country house. Yes, sometimes the most delicious treat for moments like this is a warming drink. You will find tasty snacks to go with these drinks on page 63.

WHITE GLOGG WITH VANILLA VODKA

Approximately 34 Oz.

1 bottle of dry white wine
1/2 cup brown sugar
1 tsp. whole cardamom pods
2 tbsp. sliced fresh ginger
12 cloves
2 cinnamon sticks
4 tbsp. Absolut Vanilla Vodka

Serve with
almonds and raisins

🍂 Carefully heat wine, sugar, and spices without boiling them. Remove the pan from the heat.

🍂 Cover and let it stand like this for a few hours. Strain to remove the spices.

🍂 Add the liquor and heat the glogg carefully when it is time to drink it. Don't let it boil.

WINE PUNCH WITH APPLE AND TANGERINE

Approximately 34 Oz.

1 bottle of dry white wine
1 cup apple juice concentrate
5 tbsp. raw sugar
2 cinnamon sticks
10 cloves
3 tbsp. Absolut Mandrin
2 clementines or 1 orange

🍂 Carefully heat the wine, juice, sugar, and spices without boiling. Remove the pan from the heat.

🍂 Cover and let it sit for a few hours. Strain to remove the spices.

🍂 Add the alcohol and heat the punch carefully when it is time to drink it. Don't let it boil.

🍂 Rinse the citrus fruit and cut into smaller pieces. Add them to the punch.

HOT JUNIPER BERRY AND BITTER ORANGE DRINK

Approximately 3 1/2 Cups

1 1/3 cups water
12 juniper berries
3 bitter orange peels, whole
1 bottle of dry white wine
1/2 cup honey
4 tbsp. gin

🍂 Boil water, juniper berries, and bitter orange peels covered for 10 minutes. Strain to remove the spices.

🍂 Mix the spiced water with wine, honey, and gin in a skillet. Heat the punch carefully without boiling it.

NORDIC GLÜHWEIN

Approximately 50 Oz.

2 blood oranges or regular oranges
1 lemon
1 3/4 cups concentrated lingonberry juice
34 oz. water
3–4 tbsp. raw sugar
3 cinnamon sticks
0.5 cup Explorer Lingon Blueberry
or plain vodka

🍂 Squeeze the juice out of the citrus fruits.

🍂 Carefully heat the citrus juice, the lingonberry juice, water, sugar, and cinnamon. Remove the pan from the heat.

🍂 Cover and let it sit for a few hours.
🍂 Add the alcohol and heat the punch carefully, but don't let it boil.

SNACKS

December is a hectic month for most of us. During this fast-paced frenzy, it feels good to invite friends over for casual quality time on a weekend. Snacks, glogg, and good conversation simply brighten the dark winter days. The sweet glogg or any other warming drink (page 61) is excellent with flavorful cheeses. The treats below are the usual choice for one of those nights.

DATE YUMMIES

25 Pieces

25 dates, preferably fresh
3.5 oz. aged cheese (preferably Västerbotten cheese)

🍃 Make a cut in the date and remove the seed.

🍃 Cut the cheese into smaller pieces. Fill each date with a piece of cheese.

BLUE CHEESE BALLS

Approximately 30 Pieces

8.8 oz. blue cheese
4.4 oz. cottage cheese
8–10 gingerbread cookies

🍃 Mix the blue cheese and the cottage cheese into a mushy medley. Allow it to firm up in the fridge and shape into balls.

🍃 Roll the balls in crushed gingerbread cookies and store in the fridge until it is time to serve them.

CHEESE STICKS

Approximately 35 Sticks

5.3 oz. seed-spiced cheese or other aged cheese
heaping 1/2 cup wheat flour
1/4 tsp. salt
7 tbsp. cold butter
1 tbsp. cold water
1 whisked egg

🍃 Grate the cheese, preferably in a food processor. Take out a third of the grated cheese and set it aside. Leave the rest of it in the food processor.

🍃 Cut the butter into small pieces and combine with the flour and salt. Mix for a few seconds. Add the water and mix until the batter starts to shape into a ball. Store the dough in the fridge for at least 1 hour.

🍃 Heat the oven to 425°F. Roll the dough into a rectangle that is 14 × 4 inches and that is about 1/4 inches thick. Brush with the lightly beaten egg and spread the rest of the cheese on top. Cut the dough into 1/2-inch-thick strips.

🍃 Place the cheese sticks on parchment-paper-covered baking trays. Bake in the middle of the oven for approximately 10 minutes.

BLUE CHEESE CANAPÉS

Approximately 30 Canapés

1 package of German wholemeal bread, 17.5 oz.
7 oz. blue cheese
1 stick plus 3 tbsp. butter (room temperature)
1.8 oz. finely chopped walnut kernels

🍃 Cut off the edges of the bread.

🍃 Mix blue cheese and butter in a food processor. Mix in the nuts.

🍃 Layer the bread slices with thick layers of cheese in between. Start and finish with a piece of bread and gently press down. Cover in plastic wrap and then in aluminum foil. Carefully press again so that cheese and bread are stuck together.

🍃 Put a weight on top to press the bread even more. Let it stand like that for at least 24 hours. It will stay fresh for 3–4 days. Slice the bread thinly before serving. Then cut the slices diagonally to make triangles.

FISH AND SEAFOOD

The produce comes from our clear waters, abundant forests, and beautiful gardens.
Seasoned with the spices in nature around us—dill, horseradish, allspice,
juniper berries—eating from our local pantry is both wise and exciting.

WHITEFISH SALAD WITH EGG AND HORSERADISH

4 Portions

2 eggs
8.8 oz. green asparagus
7 oz. cooked cold new potatoes
1 red onion
1 bunch of radishes
1/2 cucumber
1 small head iceberg lettuce
8.8 oz. smoked and cleaned whitefish
1/4 cup chopped dill

Dressing

3 tbsp. cold-pressed rapeseed oil
2 tbsp. fresh-squeezed lemon juice
1 tbsp. grated horseradish
salt

This is a true summer salad with early-harvest vegetables like asparagus and new potatoes.

❧ Begin by mixing all the ingredients for the dressing.

❧ Boil the eggs for approximately 6 minutes; the yolks should preferably be slightly creamy. Rinse in cold water and divide the eggs in the middle.

❧ Cut off the bottom coarser part of the asparagus. Boil until soft in lightly salted water, about 4 minutes. Cool the asparagus in cold water.

❧ Cut the asparagus in the middle and cut the potatoes into smaller pieces. Slice the onion and the radishes. Peel the cucumber in stripes. Divide it along the long side, scrape away the seeds, and cut into slices. Break the lettuce into smaller pieces.

❧ Mix salad, potatoes, and vegetables, and put whitefish and eggs on top. Drizzle with dressing and garnish with dill.

CREAMY SALMON AND PASTA SALAD

4 Portions

7oz.–10 oz. gravlax
10 oz. pasta
3/4 cup sliced radishes
1/3 cup sliced celery
2 tbsp. capers

Dressing

1 cup plain yogurt
grated zest from 1/4 orange
2 tbsp. freshly squeezed orange juice
1/3 cup chopped dill
2 tsp. honey (liquid)
1 tbsp. coarse-grained mustard
salt and freshly ground white pepper

This is absolutely perfect in the picnic basket. Don't forget to bring a delicious loaf of bread and a bottle of chilled white wine.

❧ Mix the ingredients for the dressing and add salt and pepper.

❧ Cook the pasta according to the instructions on the package, strain, and let it cool off a bit.

❧ Pour the dressing on top and mix.

❧ Mix radishes, celery, and capers with the pasta. Cut the salmon into strips and carefully mix into the salad.

Perch packet charr with wild butter

PERCH PACKETS

21 oz. perch fillets
2 carrots
2 beets
1 fennel
salt and freshly ground white pepper
12 anchovy fillets
2 tsp. liquid from the anchovy fillets
1/2 cup chopped dill
2 tbsp. butter

Serve with
freshly grated horseradish
cooked potatoes

You can prepare the fish packets way ahead of time and just stick them in the oven when the time comes. In the summer, you should put them on the grill of course!

🍃 Heat the oven to 400°F. Grease 4 sheets of aluminum foil. Peel carrots and beets. Cut the root vegetables in strips as skinny as matches. Clean the fennel and cut it into strips.

🍃 Spread the vegetables over the foil sheets. Season the fish with salt and pepper and place it on top of the vegetables.

🍃 Place three anchovy fillets on top of each fish fillet and drip some of the anchovy liquid on top. Spread some dill and a bit of butter on top.

🍃 Fold the packets and make sure that the edges are closed so that the liquid does not seep through. Place the packets on a tray and bake in the oven for 20 minutes. Serve with horseradish and potatoes.

CHARR WITH WILD BUTTER

4 charr fillets with the skin, each 5.3 oz.
1/2 tsp. salt
1 ml white pepper
butter for sautéing

Wild Butter
5 tbsp. butter (room temperature)
8 crushed juniper berries
1 1/2 tbsp. thyme leaves
salt and freshly ground white pepper

On our latitudes we can enjoy fish from cold streams. Cooking fish the Swedish way means letting the natural flavors dominate and just enhancing them a bit with our own spices. Mashed potatoes with chanterelles are just right with this fish.

🍃 Mix the ingredients for the spiced butter. Put it in a bowl and let it firm up in the fridge.

🍃 Season the fish with salt and pepper. Allow the butter to turn light brown in a skillet. Place the fish in it with the skin side turned down and lower the heat. Sauté on low heat for about 10 minutes. Turn the fish and sauté until cooked, about 1–2 minutes.

CHANTERELLE MASH

10–12 potatoes (floury kind, i.e., King Edward)
7 oz. chanterelles
butter
salt and freshly ground white pepper
1 cup milk

🍃 Peel the potatoes and cut into smaller pieces. Boil until soft in lightly salted water, approximately 15 minutes. Pour out the water.

🍃 Sauté chanterelles in butter until the liquid is absorbed. Season with salt and pepper.

🍃 Heat the milk. Mash the potatoes with an electric mixer. Mix the mash with the warm milk and whisk it until fluffy.

🍃 Mix in the mushrooms and season with salt and pepper.

10 oz. chanterelles
7 oz. small fresh onions
butter
1 ml freshly ground caraway seeds
salt and freshly ground white pepper
1 cup water with 1/2 cube
of chicken bouillon
1 cup cream
17.5 oz. freshly cooked new potatoes
1 jar crayfish tails in pickle, 12.7 oz.
3 tbsp. chopped dill

Serve with
freshly sautéed fish

CRAYFISH PAN WITH CHANTERELLES

Place potatoes, sauce, and vegetables all in the same pan. Serve with freshly sautéed fish.

🐟 Clean the chanterelles and cut the bigger pieces into smaller pieces. Peel the onions.

🐟 Sauté mushrooms and onions in butter until the onion until soft but not yet brown. Season with caraway, salt, and pepper.

🐟 Pour broth and cream into the pan and let it boil. Mix in the potatoes and continue cooking for a few minutes.

🐟 Strain the crayfish tails and add them to the mix with some dill.

4 portion sizes of fresh codfish,
each 5.3 oz.
3 tbsp. salt
3 1/2 cups water with 1 cube vegetable
bouillon
a few sprigs of parsley
a few sprigs of fresh thyme
1 parsnip, cut into staffs
1 large carrot, cut into staffs
2 potatoes, cut into wedges
2 inches of leek, shredded
a few leaves of savoy cabbage,
cut into pieces
salt and freshly ground white pepper

Serve with
horseradish aioli
a delicious farmhouse bread

POT-AU-FEU WITH CODFISH

Briskly season the cod with salt so that it acquires a nice white color and beautiful texture. A bit of horse-radish will give it a delicious kick.

🐟 Carefully place the pieces of cod on a plate, sprinkle with salt, and let stand at room temperature for approximately 1 hour. Turn the fish a time or two.

🐟 Boil water, bouillon, and herb sprigs in a low, wide pan. Cover and let it simmer for 5 minutes. Lift out the herbs.

🐟 Place root vegetables and potatoes in the broth, cover with a lid, and simmer about 10 minutes. Add leek and savoy cabbage and continue to cook for 5 minutes. Lift out the vegetables and keep them warm.

🐟 Quickly rinse the cod and place in the barely boiling broth. Let it stand for 5–7 minutes covered with a lid. Season with salt and pepper.

🐟 Put the vegetables back into the pan and allow them to heat up again.

2 yolks
1 cup cold-pressed rapeseed oil
1 tbsp. freshly grated horseradish
salt

HORSERADISH AIOLI

It is important that all the ingredients are at a room temperature.

🐟 Beat the yolks in a food processor or a bowl.

🐟 Add the oil, drop by drop, while beating the eggs. Don't pour the oil too quickly; the yolks need to absorb the oil or they will split.

🐟 Season with horseradish and salt and allow the flavors to mature in the fridge for at least 1 hour.

Crayfish pan with chanterelles

Pot-au-feu with codfish

SCAMPI WITH DILL

The ocean holds a very important place in the soul of many people, and many of us love fish and seafood.

8 cooked Norway lobsters

Spiced Butter
3 tbsp. butter (room temperature)
1 tsp. freshly ground dill seeds
2 tsp. coarse-grained mustard
3 tbsp. chopped dill
salt and freshly ground white pepper

Serve with
a fresh loaf of bread

🦐 Mix the ingredients for the spiced butter.

🦐 Heat the oven to 475–525°. Split the Norway lobsters lengthwise and place them on a parchment-paper–covered baking tray.

🦐 Spread the butter on the lobsters and bake on the top rack of the oven for approximately 4 minutes.

CLAM POT WITH SMOKED PORK

Blue mussels are inexpensive and festive, and they make the perfect meal for guests. Simple, beautiful, and delicious. Serve with a tasty, fresh bread to soak up the savory sauce.

2 net bags of fresh blue mussels
approximately 5.3 oz. smoked bacon
2 shallots
butter
1 1/3 cups dry white wine
freshly ground white pepper
1 cup whipping cream
1 cup chopped parsley
1 cup chopped dill

Serve with
a fresh loaf of bread

🦐 *Clean the mussels.* Brush them under running cold water, pull off the beard, and scrape away the dirt. Throw away the mussels that are open and that do not close up when you knock on them.

🦐 Cut the bacon into small cubes. Peel and chop the onion. Fry the bacon and onion in the butter in a pot. Pour in the wine, and season with freshly ground pepper.

🦐 Put the mussels in the pot and cover with a lid. Let them boil until they open up, about 5 minutes. Throw away the mussels that do not open up when cooked.

🦐 Add the cream and give it a quick boil before you add the herbs.

COD BURGERS WITH ANCHOVY DRESSING

6 Burgers

21 oz, fresh codfish fillets
2 eggs
1 big bunch of chives (chopped)
1 tsp, salt
1 ml freshly ground white pepper
butter for sautéing
1 small can of anchovy fillets, 2 oz.
1 cup light crème fraîche
3 tbsp. chopped dill
6 hamburger buns
white pepper for the sauce
shredded salad
sliced tomato

You can cook these cod burgers using frozen or fresh fish; they will taste just as delicious either way. The children might not find the anchovy dressing as tasty, but try replacing the anchovies with 3 tablespoons Kalles caviar.

❧ Cut cod fillets into small cubes. Mix fish, eggs, half of the chives, salt, and pepper.

❧ Shape the mixture into six burgers. Fry them golden brown in butter, about 4 minutes on each side.

❧ Chop the anchovies and mix with sour cream, dill, and the rest of the chives. Season the dressing with freshly ground black pepper.

❧ Warm the bread slightly in the oven. Add fish burgers, lettuce, tomato, and dressing on the buns and serve immediately.

SALMON-FILLED HERRING WITH MUSTARD MASH

4 Portions

21 oz. herring fillet
1 tsp. salt
1 ml freshly ground white pepper
3.5 oz. cold-smoked salmon, thinly sliced
3 tbsp. chopped dill
1 egg
scant 1/3 cup coarse rye flour

Herring is an inexpensive and delicious everyday fish that is easily forgotten. A bit of smoked salmon will enhance its flavor. Mustard mash complements this dish.

❧ Rinse herring fillets, drain, and dry them thoroughly. Cut off the dorsal fin. Place the herring on a cutting board with the fleshy side up and season with salt and pepper.

❧ Add a piece of salmon on half of the herring fillets and sprinkle with dill. Add remaining fillets on top.

❧ Turn herring in lightly beaten egg and flour. Allow the butter to turn light brown and sauté herring fillets golden brown on both sides.

MUSTARD MASH

4 Portions

10–12 potatoes (starchy kind, such as King Edward)
1 cup milk
1 tbsp. butter
3 tbsp. coarse-grain mustard
salt and freshly ground white pepper

❧ Peel potatoes and cut into smaller pieces. Boil in lightly salted water until soft, about 15 minutes. Drain.

❧ Heat the milk. Mash the potatoes with an electric mixer. Mix the mash with warm milk, butter, and mustard and beat until fluffy. Season with salt and pepper.

Cod burger with anchovy dressing

Salmon-filled herring with mustard mash

PASTA AND SALMON PUDDING

5 cups cooked macaroni, cold
14 oz. smoked salmon slices
3 eggs
1 1/3 cups milk
salt and freshly ground white pepper
1 tbsp. cold pressed rapeseed oil
1 clove garlic, pressed
7–10 oz. fresh baby spinach
1 cup green peas
1/4 cup grated cheese

A mix between salmon pudding and macaroni. Two classics in one delectable dish.

❧ Preheat the oven to 400°F. Whisk eggs, milk, and salt and pepper lightly.

❧ Heat oil and garlic in a sauté pan, add the spinach, and cook until the spinach is just wilted. Add salt and pepper.

❧ Add half of the cooked pasta and peas in a greased ovenproof dish. Add the spinach, salmon, and peas and finish off with the rest of the pasta.

❧ Pour the egg mixture into the dish and sprinkle with cheese. Bake in the middle of the oven, about 30 minutes.

PIZZA WITH SALMON AND DILL OIL

0.9 oz. yeast
scant 1 cup lukewarm water
1 tbsp. cold-pressed rapeseed oil
1/2 tsp. salt
1 3/4–2 cups sifted spelt flour
or wheat flour

Filling
7 oz. cold-smoked salmon, thinly sliced
1/2 squash
1 red onion
10 oz. grated aged cheese, such as grevé
16 cherry tomatoes

Dill Oil
1/2 cup cold-pressed rapeseed oil
2 pressed garlic cloves
1/2 cup finely chopped dill

I usually use spelt flour in my pizza dough. It's healthier than white flour and tastes great. Whatever I choose to put on top of my pizza depends on my mood, but it is delightfully refreshing with smoked salmon, vegetables, and dill oil.

🌿 Dissolve yeast in water. Add oil, salt, and flour. Work into a smooth dough. Let rise covered under a cloth for about 30 minutes.

🌿 Mix the ingredients for the dill oil.

🌿 Slice squash and onion thinly.

🌿 Preheat the oven to 475°F (you can bake two sheets with all four pizzas simultaneously in a convection oven). Divide the dough into four parts and roll them out into 7-inch large circles. Transfer the circles, two by two, to a baking sheet. In the meantime, heat one or two baking trays in the oven.

🌿 Drizzle a little bit of dill oil over the pizza circles. Sprinkle on cheese and add the vegetables and a few more drops of oil.

🌿 Drag the baking sheet with the pizzas onto the heated baking trays. Bake in middle of oven for 10–15 minutes.

🌿 Take out the pizzas, top them off with slices of salmon, and drizzle the remaining oil over them.

Poached halibut with beet broth   Sautéed walleye with lentil hash

POACHED HALIBUT WITH BEET BROTH

4 Servings

4 portions halibut, 5.3 oz. each
1 carrot
4 beets
1 wedge of white cabbage
1 yellow onion
5.3 oz. smoked bacon
butter for sautéeing
34 oz. chicken broth
2 bay leaves
a few sprigs of fresh thyme
2 tbsp. apple cider vinegar
salt and freshly ground white pepper

Serve with
1 wedge of savoy cabbage,
3 tbsp butter
1/2 tsp. freshly ground caraway seeds
1.8 oz. black roe
4 tbsp. freshly grated horseradish
cooked potatoes

Beautiful red broth, white fish, and a dollop of black rum. What a presentation!

❧ Peel and grate the carrot, the beets, and the cabbage coarsely. Chop the onion and bacon. Fry the vegetables and pork in butter until cooked but not browned, about 10 minutes.

❧ Add broth and spices, cover with a lid, and cook for about 30 minutes. Strain and pour the broth back into the saucepan. Bring to a boil and season with vinegar, salt, and pepper.

❧ Poach the fish under a cover in lightly salted water until it is thoroughly cooked and the flesh is white and firm. Use a thermometer; the fish is ready when it shows 129°F; it takes about 10 minutes.

❧ Shred savoy cabbage and sauté in butter until soft. Season with freshly ground caraway.

❧ Spread cabbage in deep plates and pour beet broth inside.

❧ Add the fish and top with rum and horseradish. Serve with boiled potatoes.

SAUTÉED WALLEYE WITH LENTIL HASH

4 Servings

21 oz. of walleye fillets
1 tsp. salt
1/4 cup coarse rye flour
butter for sautéeing

Lentil Hash
5.3 oz. smoked bacon
1 leek
2 cans of lentils, each 14 oz.
butter
7 oz. fresh baby spinach
salt and freshly ground white pepper

Sour Cream Sauce
1 1/3 cups sour cream
1/3 cup chopped dill
2 tbsp. coarse-grained mustard
salt

Hash with the fish? Sure, but I replace the potatoes with lentils and spinach. And I mix in a bit of bacon, the Norwegian way.

❧ Mix the ingredients for the sauce.

❧ *Hash.* Shred the pork. Rinse and slice the leeks. Rinse lentils in cold water and let them drain.

❧ Fry the pork in a dab of butter in a large pan (if you use a nonstick pan, you can skip the butter). Add the leek and let it fry for a while.

❧ Reduce the heat and mix in the lentils and lastly the spinach. The spinach will probably be overflowing the pan at first, but it collapses in an instant. Season with salt and pepper.

❧ *Fish.* Salt the fish and turn it in the flour. Sauté in butter in a frying pan until it is golden brown and thoroughly cooked.

SALMON À LA SKAGEN WITH ROE

4 Servings

4 servings of salmon, 5.3 oz. each
1.8 oz. roe

Filling
5.3 oz. peeled shrimp
3 tbsp. light sour cream
3 tbsp. mayonnaise
1/3 cup chopped dill
1 pinch cayenne pepper

Tore Wretman's skagen medley is a classic in our Swedish food culture. Here I bake the salmon with the medley and top it off with roe. Perfect for a party. In the summer I serve it with primeur salad, but in the winter it is good with mashed potatoes.

❧ Preheat the oven to 425°F. Make a deep incision all the way to the skin in the center of each salmon piece so that you get a pocket. Make sure that you do not cut through skin and that each piece holds together at both ends.

❧ Chop the shrimp coarsely and mix with remaining ingredients for the filling. Distribute the filling in the pockets. Place the salmon on a baking tray with parchment paper.

❧ Bake the salmon in the center of the oven for 12–15 minutes. Top the pieces off with a splash of rum.

PRIMEUR SALAD

4 Servings

17.5 oz. new potatoes
8.8 oz. green asparagus
3.5 oz. sugar snap peas
1/3 cup chopped spring onion

Dressing
3 tbsp. rapeseed oil
2 tbsp. fresh lemon juice
2 tsp. coarse-grained mustard
salt and freshly ground white pepper

❧ Brush the potatoes and boil in lightly salted water. Break off the rough bottom area of the asparagus stalks. Boil the asparagus until tender in salted water, about 4 minutes. Divide stalks in the middle. Blanch the sugar snap peas in lightly salted water.

❧ Mix the ingredients for the dressing.

❧ Drain the vegetables and mix them with the dressing.

MEAT AND CHICKEN

The short days, the darkness, and all the candles—
the dark winter season has a very special atmosphere.
Our rhythm of life tends to slow down, and we like to stay closer to home.
Our habits and cravings change, and so does our cooking.

ROOT VEGETABLE LOBSCOUSE

1 turnip, 28 oz.
2 large carrots
2 parsnips
1 piece celeriac, about 7 oz.
34 oz. water with 2 cubes
of vegetable bouillon
8 potatoes of a starchy variety, such as
King Edward
2 tbsp. butter
3/4 tsp. freshly ground allspice
salt
1 can of corned beef, 12 oz.

Serve with
pickled beets
coarse-grained mustard

Lobscouse used to be one of my favorite dishes at school. Now I love to cook it with root vegetables.

❧ Peel the root vegetables and cut into smaller pieces. Boil them in the broth, about 20 minutes.

❧ Peel potatoes and cut into small pieces. Add the potatoes and continue cooking until all root vegetables are tender, about 15 minutes.

❧ Pour out the broth, but save about 1 cup of it.

❧ Mash the vegetables with an old-fashioned potato masher or a wooden fork. Dilute the broth to suitable consistency. Add pats of butter and season with allspice and salt.

❧ Tear the meat with a fork into the mash, mix, and heat.

BARLEY RISOTTO WITH CRISPY BACON

1 1/3 cups barley
1 onion
about 10 oz. fresh mushrooms
butter
about 5 cups boiling hot water with 2
vegetable bouillon cubes
1 cup coarsely grated priest cheese,
or other aged cheese
1/3 cup chopped parsley
freshly ground black pepper

Roasted Beets
17.5 oz. beets
1 1/2 tbsp. cold-pressed rapeseed oil
2 tsp. thyme
gourmet salt

Serve with
crispy bacon

Among all the new grains that have come from distant lands, our own barley defends its position well. In the past, barley porridge was considered a simple meal. Now, barley is trendy. Here I have cooked barley and pork with a modern twist.

❧ *Risotto.* Chop the onion and cut the mushrooms into small pieces. Sauté in butter in a pot until soft but not browned. Stir in the barley and let the grains fry for a while until they become glazed.

❧ Pour in enough broth to cover the grains. Let the broth boil. Continue cooking the risotto this way: Dilute with a little liquid at a time and let it absorb before more is added. Stir regularly. Cook until the grains are tender, about 35 minutes.

❧ Mix in cheese and parsley and season with pepper. Let the risotto stand covered for 3–5 minutes. If necessary, dilute with more water; the risotto should be creamy.

❧ *Beets.* Preheat the oven to 425°F. Brush the beets clean and cut them into smaller pieces. Place them on a baking tray with parchment paper and mix with oil and thyme.

❧ Roast beets in the center of the oven until tender, about 30 minutes. Stir every once in a while. Season with salt.

Dressing
2 tbsp. cold-pressed rapeseed oil
1 tbsp. fresh lemon juice
2 tbsp. grated horseradish
2 tbsp. chopped chives
salt

Serve with
sautéed coarsely ground smoked sausage
mashed potatoes

SMOKED SAUSAGE WITH WARM BEET SALAD

Smoked sausage with pickled beets, what a yummy combination! But I am crazy about fresh beets, and combined with the horseradish dressing, they kick some serious taste buds with the sautéed sausage.

❧ Preheat the oven to 425°F. Brush the beets clean and cut them into wedges. Place them on a baking tray with parchment paper and drizzle with oil.

❧ Roast beets in the middle of the oven until tender, about 30 minutes. Stir every once in a while during the roasting.

❧ Stir the ingredients for the dressing and mix with the beets.

4 Servings

2 yellow onions
2.2 lb. potatoes, of a starchy variety, such as King Edward
butter
salt
3 bay leaves
1 cup hot water with 1 beef bouillon cube
1 bottle of dark beer, 11 oz.
1/3 cup chopped parsley

SAILOR POTATOES

I usually make my sailor steak without the meat. This gives me an opportunity to vary what I want to eat with it—hamburger, pork chops, meatballs, sautéed sausage. But pickles are an absolute must no matter what you choose to add to your own variation.

❧ Peel and slice onions thinly. Peel and cut potatoes into 1/2-inch-thick slices.

❧ Sauté the onions in butter. Layer the onions and potatoes in a pot, adding a little bit of salt in between the layers, and add the bay leaves.

❧ Dissolve the bouillon cube in water. Pour the broth and the beer into the pot.

❧ Let it stew and simmer with lid on until the potatoes are soft, about 45 minutes. Sprinkle with parsley.

CHICKEN WITH ELDERFLOWER

A great summer dish that is delightful with a glass of chilled white wine.

4 Servings

17.5 oz. chicken	*Marinade*
butter	*1 cup concentrated elderflower drink*
salt and freshly ground white	*3 tbsp. cold-pressed rapeseed oil*
pepper	*2 1/2 tbsp. apple cider vinegar*
	1/3 cup chopped mint
	1/3 cup chopped dill
	salt and freshly ground white pepper

❧ Preheat the oven to 325°F. Sauté chicken briefly in butter so that the outsides brown. Season with salt and pepper. Put it in an ovenproof dish in the middle of the oven and bake until the chicken is thoroughly cooked, about 15 minutes. Let the chicken cool slightly and place it in a narrow bowl.

❧ Mix the ingredients for the marinade. Pour it over the chicken. Let it marinate in the refrigerator for a few hours or overnight.

❧ Cut the chicken into thin slices and serve it with the melon salad.

MELON SALAD

4 Servings

2 wedges of honeydew melon	1 red onion
2 wedges of muskmelon	freshly squeezed juice from 1/2 lemon
1/2 cucumber	2 tbsp. cold-pressed rapeseed oil
salt and freshly	3 tbsp. chopped dill
ground white pepper	

❧ Cut the melons into small cubes. Divide the cucumber lengthwise, scrape out the seeds, and cut into small cubes. Peel and finely chop the onion.

❧ Mix the ingredients for the salad.

CHICKEN WITH BEET PESTO

Chicken fillets in beautiful fall colors.

4 Servings

4 chicken fillets
butter for sautéing
salt and freshly ground black pepper

Beet Pesto	*Hash*
5.3 oz. cooked and peeled beets	*10 oz. mixed mushrooms*
1.8 oz. walnuts	*1 small yellow onion*
1 minced garlic clove	*17.5 oz. squash*
1 tbsp. fresh lemon juice	*1 tsp. fresh thyme*
1/2 cup grated priest cheese, or other	*butter*
aged cheese	*1/3 cup chopped parsley*
1/3 cup cold-pressed rapeseed oil	
salt and freshly ground black pepper	

❧ *The pesto.* Mix beets, walnuts, garlic, and lemon juice. Mix in the cheese and finally the oil at the end. Season with salt and pepper.

❧ *The chicken.* Preheat the oven to 325°F. Brown the outsides of the chicken fillets in butter. Add salt and pepper and place them in an ovenproof dish.

❧ Bake in the middle of the oven until they are thoroughly cooked, about 15 minutes.

❧ *The hash.* Trim the mushrooms and cut into smaller pieces. Chop the onion and slice the squash thinly. Sauté mushrooms, onion, squash, and thyme in butter, about 5 minutes. Mix in parsley and season with salt and pepper.

MEATBALLS WITH RELISH MIX

Relish and celery add a new flavor to the meatballs.

4 Servings

17.5 oz. ground beef or ground game	*Sauce*
3 tbsp. chopped browned onions	*1 cup light sour cream, suitable for*
1 egg	*cooking*
3 tbsp. cream cheese	*1 tbsp. veal stock*
1/2 cup relish	*1/2 tsp. soy sauce*
1/2 cup finely chopped celery	*2 tbsp. jelly, i.e., rowanberry*
1 1/2 tsp. thyme	*1/2 cup finely diced apple or pear*
3/4 tsp. salt	
1 pinch freshly ground black pepper	*Serve with*
butter for sautéing	*boiled or mashed potatoes*

🍃 Mix the ingredients for the mince until it is smooth. Wet hands with cold water and shape into small meatballs. Place them on a cutting board that has been rinsed with water.

🍃 Brown the meatballs, a few at a time, in butter. Shake the pan so that they are evenly cooked. Reduce the heat and cook for another 3–5 minutes. Shake occasionally.

🍃 *The sauce.* Boil sour cream, stock, soy sauce, and jelly. Mix fruit cubes in the sauce.

FOREST BOLOGNESE

Who doesn't love meat sauce? My version includes a lot of root vegetables and mushrooms. Perhaps a good way to get kids to eat vegetables?

4 Servings

17.5 oz. ground beef or ground game	*1 can chopped tomatoes, 14 oz.*
meat	*1 cup game stock with chanterelle*
1 yellow onion	*10 crushed juniper berries*
3.5 oz. turnip	*1 tbsp. thyme*
3.5 oz. celeriac	*salt and freshly ground black pepper*
1 carrot	
butter	*Serve with*
5.3 oz. of fresh mixed mushrooms	*pasta*

🍃 Peel and chop the onion. Peel the root vegetables and cut them into small cubes.

🍃 Fry onions and root vegetables in butter in a stock pot. Raise heat, add ground beef and mushrooms, and fry until the mince is crumbly.

🍃 Add tomatoes, stock, and herbs. Cover the pot and simmer for about 25 minutes. Season with salt and pepper.

ROWANBERRY CHICKEN

When I was a kid, we often got sautéed chicken with cream sauce on Sundays. This is a modern variation that's quick enough to cook any day of the week.

4 Servings

17 1/2 oz. chicken
1 leek
butter
1 cup of cream
2 tbsp. game stock with chanterelles
1/2 tsp. soy sauce
8 crushed juniper berries
3 tbsp. rowanberry jelly
salt and freshly ground black pepper

Serve with
boiled or pressed potatoes
cooked vegetables, i.e., brussels sprouts

🍂 Cut the chicken fillets into slices. Rinse and slice the leeks.

🍂 Brown the chicken in butter in a frying pan. Season with salt and pepper.

🍂 Add cream, stock, soy sauce, and juniper berries. Cover and cook the stew for approximately 5 minutes.

🍂 Stir in the leek and jelly and cook for another 5 minutes.

QUICK STEW

Here's a rapid variation of beef stew—with minute steak.

4 servings

17 1/2 oz. minute steak
2 carrots
1 leek
2 tbsp. butter
1 1/2 tbsp. flour
8 allspice berries
4 bay leaves
1 tsp. soy sauce
1 3/4 cups water with 1 1/2 tbsp. veal stock

Serve with
boiled potatoes
pickled beets

🍂 Cut the meat into strips. Peel carrots and slice them thinly. Rinse and slice the leek.

🍂 Brown the meat in butter in a frying pan. Stir in flour and add carrots, leek, spices, soy sauce, and stock.

🍂 Cover with a lid and boil the stew for approximately 10 minutes. Personally, I think the saltiness of the stock and the soy sauce is enough, but taste the stew to determine whether you want to add a dash of salt.

4 Servings

2.2 lb. rack of lamb
butter
1 tbsp. thyme
salt and freshly ground black pepper

Cheese Crème
3 1/2 oz. finely grated schnapps cheese,
Västerbotten cheese, or other well-aged
cheese
1 cup light crème fraîche
2 × 1 ml freshly ground fennel seeds
2 tbsp. thyme leaves
2 tbsp. vodka
salt and freshly ground white pepper

Roasted Root Vegetables
2.2 lb. mixed root vegetables, such as
carrots, beets, parsnips, celeriac, and
rutabaga
2 tbsp. rapeseed oil
1 tbsp. thyme
gourmet salt

RACK OF LAMB AND CHEESE CRÈME WITH A HINT OF VODKA

Easy to cook in the oven, easy to slice, juicy, and delicious. Roasted root vegetables are many people's favorites with a meal, and they are beautiful and healthy.

🍃 *The meat.* Preheat the oven to 325°F. Brown the rack of lamb's meaty sides in butter. Rub the meat with thyme, salt, and pepper.

🍃 Place the racks of lamb in a small roasting pan. Insert a meat thermometer into the thickest part of the meat, but make sure that it does not touch the bones.

🍃 Roast the meat in the middle of the oven until the thermometer shows 140°F and the meat is pink inside. It takes about 20 minutes.

🍃 Wrap meat in aluminum foil and let it rest for 10–15 minutes. That will even out the temperature and ensure that the meat doesn't spill too much gravy. Cut the meat in between each bone.

🍃 *The cheese crème.* Mix the ingredients and let the flavors mature a while before serving.

🍃 *The root vegetables.* Preheat the oven to 425°F. Brush the vegetables clean and peel the celeriac and turnip. Cut into smaller pieces. Place them on a baking sheet with parchment paper and mix with oil and thyme.

🍃 Roast the vegetables in the middle of the oven until tender, about 30 minutes. Stir occasionally. Season with salt.

JUNIPER BERRY BURGER WITH LINGON COLESLAW

Hamburgers are always a treat. And since I have a taste for wild meat, my burgers turn out like this.

21 oz. ground game or ground beef
1 egg
3/4 tsp. salt
1 pinch freshly ground black pepper
6 crushed juniper berries
1 tsp. thyme

🌿 Mix the ingredients into a smooth mince and shape into four burgers.

🌿 Grill the burgers on the grill iron pan or sauté them in butter.

Serve with
lingon coleslaw
chantarelle mash (p. 71)

14 oz. cabbage
about 68 oz. water
1 carrot
1/2 red onion
1/3 cup lingonberries
1/3 cup sour cream
3 tbsp. mayonnaise
1 tsp. vinegar essence, 12 percent
salt and freshly ground white pepper

LINGON COLESLAW

🌿 Shred the cabbage thinly with a cheese slicer and place it in a colander. Boil water and pour over cabbage. Drain thoroughly and squeeze out all water.

🌿 Grate carrots coarsely and slice onion thinly.

🌿 Mix all the ingredients and let the flavors mature for a few moments before serving..

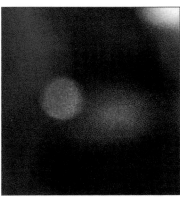

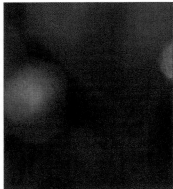

about 3 lb. boneless venison or other wild
meat, pieces such as rump steak, flank,
or roast beef
1/3 cup soy sauce
1/3 cup undiluted black currant juice
1 bottle of stout, 11 oz.
2 tbsp. game stock with chanterelle
1 large yellow onion, cut into wedges
8 crushed juniper berries
10 black peppercorns
1 tsp. dried thyme

Cream Sauce
3 1/2 cups from the cooking stock
scant 1 cup cream
4 tbsp. flour
3 tbsp. rowanberry or currant jelly

Serve with
roasted root vegetables (p. 100)
cucumber salad

WILD ROAST WITH STOUT

We must not lose our traditions. It is time to reinstate the Sunday steak! And what would a good steak be without the classic cream sauce and pickled cucumber salad?

🌿 Tie up the meat with twine.

🌿 Pour soy sauce, juice, stout, and stock in a pan that holds the meat snugly. Add the onion and spices.

🌿 Add the roast and boil. Reduce heat, cover with a lid, and cook on low heat for approximately 1 1/2 hours. Baste the roast a few times during this period. If you are using a thermometer, insert it in the thickest part of the meat. The roast is ready at 167°F. Let it rest in the broth for at least 15 minutes. Lift the roast out of the pan and wrap it in aluminum foil.

🌿 *The sauce.* Strain and measure the cooking stock, possibly dilute it with water to get 3 1/2 cups. Bring cooking stock and cream to a boil. Mix the flour with 1/3 cup water. Whisk into the sauce to thicken it and cook for about 5 minutes. Stir in the jelly and taste.

🌿 Cut the steak into very thin slices and serve with gravy, roasted root vegetables, and cucumber salad.

1 fresh cucumber
3 × 1 ml salt
2 tbsp. vinegar essence, 12 percent
1/3 cup water
2 tbsp. granulated sugar
1/2 pinch freshly ground white pepper
2 tbsp. chopped parsley

CUCUMBER SALAD

🌿 Slice the cucumber thinly with a cheese slicer. Put it in a bowl, sprinkle with salt, and mix. Cover with a plate and put some sort of weight on top. Let stand for about 30 minutes.

🌿 Mix a pickle of vinegar, water, sugar, pepper, and parsley. Stir until the sugar dissolves.

🌿 Pour it over the cucumber slices. Let stand an hour or two before serving.

ELK STEW WITH ROOT VEGETABLES

There is nothing unusual about beef stew with vegetables. But here I have chosen to top it off with sautéed root vegetables and mushrooms. It is decorative and the vegetables retain a nice, firm texture.

4 Servings

28 oz. boneless elk meat or venison,
  i.e., shoulder cut or steak
2 carrots
butter
1 parsnip
14–18 oz. mixed vegetables,
such as onion, carrot,
celery, parsnips
1 3/4 cups red wine
3 cups water with 2 tbsp. game stock
  with chanterelle
2 bay leaves
1 tbsp. thyme
8 lightly crushed juniper berries
salt and freshly ground black pepper
1 tbsp. butter
1 tbsp. flour

Root Vegetables
1 large red onion
5–7 oz. mushrooms, i.e., chanterelles
butter
salt and freshly ground black pepper
1 tbsp. thyme leaves, scratched

Serve with
mashed potatoes
lingon berry jam

🦌 *The stew.* Cut the meat into smaller pieces, approximately 1 × 1 inch. Use a frying pan to brown the meat in butter, in batches. Set aside.

🦌 Peel and cut the vegetables into smaller pieces. Sauté them in butter in a saucepan. Add the wine and cook uncovered until the wine has reduced to about half.

🦌 Pour stock into the pan, add the meat, and bring to a boil and skim off the foam. Add spices and cook the stew on low heat, covered, until the meat is tender, about 1 1/4 hour.

🦌 Remove the meat and strain it from the stock. Put meat and stock back into the pot. Stir butter and flour and mix into the stew. Cook for another 5 minutes and season with salt and pepper.

🦌 *The root vegetables.* Peel and cut carrots and parsnips into thin rods, cut the onion into wedges, and cut the mushrooms into smaller pieces. Sauté vegetables and mushrooms in butter, about 10 minutes. Season with salt and pepper and add the thyme. Top the meat stew with root vegetables and mushrooms.

LAMB STEW WITH LEGUME PUREE

It is always a pleasure to warm up to a hearty beef stew. Serve it with legume puree and you will turn it into a new and festive experience! A good bread is an absolute must, because you are going to want to soak up the delicious sauce and dip it in the legume puree.

4 Servings

28 oz. boneless lamb legume puree,
  for example, from the roast
1 can chickpeas, 14 oz.
1 1/2 tbsp. thyme
2 slices of salted bacon
2 yellow onions
2 tbsp. thyme leaves
3 large carrots
3 tbsp. rapeseed oil
3 celery stalks
about 2 tbsp. of broth from the pot
1 squash
salt and freshly ground black pepper
butter

3 bay leaves
1.7 cups dry white wine
1 1/2 tbsp. veal stock
1 cup of the vegetables from the pot
1 chopped garlic clove

Serve with
a fresh loaf of bread

🐑 Cut the meat into smaller pieces, approximately 1 1/4 × 1 1/4 inches. Roll the meat in thyme. Cut the bacon into strips. Slice onions, carrots, celery, and squash.

🐑 Sauté the bacon in butter in a saucepan, add the meat, and sear it all around. Season with salt and pepper. Add all the vegetables except for the butternut squash and let them sauté for a few minutes.

🐑 Add the bay leaves, wine, and stock. Cover with a lid and cook until the meat is tender, about 1 1/4 hours.

🐑 When you have about 30 minutes of cooking time remaining, add the squash.

🐑 *The legume puree.* Rinse the chickpeas and drain them. Mix all the ingredients, dilute with broth from the pot, and season with salt and pepper. Serve the legume puree when it is lukewarm together with the stew.

21 oz. venison fillet
1/3 cup gin
1/4 cup lingonberries
butter
salt and freshly ground black pepper

FILLET OF VENISON WITH LINGONBERRIES AND GIN

Not everyone is fortunate enough to have access to game meat. Luckily, the marinade is also good with beef tenderloin.

❧ Trim the fillet free from membranes and tendons.

❧ Pour gin and lingonberries into a plastic bag and mix. Add the fillet and tie the bag. Let it marinate in the refrigerator at least 4 hours but preferably overnight.

❧ Preheat the oven to 325°F. Take out the fillet and save the marinade.

❧ Brown the fillet all around in the butter. Season with salt and pepper.

❧ Stick a meat thermometer into the fillet and place it in an ovenproof dish. Pour the marinade over the meat.

❧ Roast fillet in the center of the oven until thermometer shows 132.8–136.4°F, about 10–15 minutes.

❧ Cover the dish with aluminum foil and let the meat stand for 10 minutes before you cut it into thin slices.

4 Servings

17 1/2 oz. potatoes of a floury variety, such as King Edward
1 large carrot
1 large parsnip
1 piece of celeriac, 3.5 oz.
1 piece of turnip, 3.5 oz.
2 pressed garlic cloves
2 tsp. thyme
1 1/2 pinches ground nutmeg
1 cup whipping cream
1/2 cup milk
1 1/2 tsp. salt
2 × 1 ml pepper
1 1/3 cups grated cheese, preferably Västerbotten cheese if possible

ROOT VEGETABLE GRATIN

Root vegetables add so much more flavor to the gratin than just plain potatoes.

❧ Preheat the oven to 425°F. Peel the potatoes and the root vegetables and slice them thinly, preferably in a food processor.

❧ Mix all the ingredients in a large bowl, but save half of the cheese. It is easiest to use your hands.

❧ Pour the mixture into an ovenproof dish and sprinkle with the remaining cheese.

❧ Bake in the middle of the oven until the vegetables are tender and the gratin is nicely browned, 45–50 minutes.

PIES AND DESSERTS

Warm freshly cooked rhubarb cream with ice-cold creamy milk.
This is the essence of summer in the country!

LIGONBERRY CHEESECAKE

8–10 Pieces

8.8 oz. graham crackers
7 tbsp. melted butter
1 tbsp. ground cinnamon

Filling
3 eggs
3 tbsp. granulated sugar
7 oz. cream cheese, room temperature
1 cup crème fraîche
2 tsp. vanilla sugar
1/3 cup lingonberry jam

Jelly
1 gelatin leaf
1/3 cup of concentrated lingonberry juice (You can also use concentrated cranberry juice.)
1/3 cup lingonberry jam

To me, lingonberries and cinnamon are typical fall and winter flavors, but they go well together any time of the year. I like to use lingonberries and lingonberry jam when baking, because the berries have a refreshing and moderately sweet taste.

❧ Crumble biscuits in a food processor. Add the melted butter and cinnamon and mix into a crumbly mass. Press the dough into a baking pan with removable bottom, 10 inches in diameter. Let it stand in the refrigerator for at least 30 minutes.

❧ Preheat the oven to 325°F. Prebake the piecrust in the middle of the oven for about 5 minutes.

❧ Beat eggs and sugar until fluffy. Whisk in the remaining ingredients.

❧ Pour filling into the pie shell and bake on the middle rack of the oven, about 35 minutes. The filling should have gelled somewhat but still be a little loose in the middle. The filling will firm up even more once it cools off. Let the pie cool.

❧ Soak the gelatin leaf in cold water for about 5 minutes. Heat the lingonberry drink and remove the pan from the heat. Remove the gelatin leaf from cold water and allow it to slowly melt in the lingonberry drink. Let the gel cool in the fridge until it has a suitable consistency that can be spooned over the pie.

❧ Spread a thin layer of jam over the pie and carefully spoon the gel over it. Cover the pie and store it in the refrigerator, preferably overnight.

CRUMB PIE WITH LINGON AND PEAR

Lingonberries and pears are a classic combination. Usually used in various preserves, but also delicious in pies.

4 Servings

Topping	Filling
1/2 cup flour	2.2 lb. pears
2/3 cup rolled oats	1/2 cup raw sugar
3 tbsp. sugar	1 1/3 cups lingonberries
7 tbsp. cold butter	2 tbsp. potato flour
	3/4 tsp. cinnamon

Serve with

vanilla ice cream or
  lightly whipped cream

☙ Preheat the oven to 425°F. Mix flour, oatmeal, and sugar. Add the butter and mix until crumbly.

☙ Peel the pears and cut each pear into six wedges. Place pears and sugar in a saucepan. Cover with a lid and let it simmer until the pears are soft but not mushy, about 8 minutes.

☙ Remove the pears from the heat. Mix in lingonberries, potato flour, and cinnamon.

☙ Pour pears, cranberries, and liquid into a greased ovenproof dish. Crumble the dough over the mix.

☙ Bake in the center of the oven, approximately 20 minutes.

CHOCOLATE CRUMB PIE

To "throw together" a crumb pie is a cinch. I vary the filling and the "crumb" according to availability and mood. I like to mix in some form of fresh berries, such as currants or gooseberries. And the crumb doesn't need to consist solely of butter and flour. Here, I have added oatmeal, hazelnuts, and dark chocolate. If you are allergic to nuts, replace them with sunflower seeds.

4 Servings

Topping	Filling
1/3 cup hazelnuts	4–6 apples
2/3 cup flour	1 cup currants or gooseberries
2/3 cup rolled oats	1/3 cup raw sugar
3 tbsp. raw sugar	2 tbsp. potato flour
3 1/2 oz. coarsely chopped	
dark chocolate	*Serve with*
7 tbsp. cold butter	*vanilla ice cream or*
	lightly whipped cream

☙ Preheat the oven to 425°F. Coarsely chop nuts. Mix nuts, flour, oatmeal, sugar, and chocolate. Add the butter and work into a crumbly mixture.

☙ Peel the apples and slice them into wedges. Layer the apple pieces, berries, sugar, and potato flour in an ovenproof dish. Crumble the dough over the filling. Bake in the center of the oven, approximately 20 minutes.

WHEY CHEESE PIE WITH HAZELNUTS

8–10 Pieces

Bottom
7 tbsp. cold butter
1 1/3 cups flour
1.8 oz. soft whey cheese
1 egg yolk

Filling
3 1/2 oz. hazelnuts
7 tbsp. melted butter
1/2 cup flour
1 cup granulated sugar
3 1/2 oz. soft whey cheese
2 egg yolks
3 egg whites

Serve with
vodka spiked berries
vanilla ice cream

It might sound a bit strange to bake a pie with soft whey cheese, but it tastes delicious. The sweet taste of the whey cheese is almost reminiscent of toffee and works very well in baking.

🌿 Chop the butter in the flour. Mix in the soft whey cheese and egg yolk and knead into a dough.

🌿 Press the dough into a baking pan with removable bottom, about 9.5 inches in diameter. Prick bottom with a fork and let the crust stand in the refrigerator for at least 30 minutes.

🌿 Preheat oven to 400°F. Prebake piecrust in the center of the oven, approximately 10 minutes.

🌿 Roast the hazelnuts in a dry, hot skillet. Rub the peel off in paper towels and chop them coarsely.

🌿 Beat butter, flour, sugar, whey, and egg yolks. Beat egg whites until stiff. Flip down the nuts and egg whites into the batter.

🌿 Pour filling into the pie shell. Bake in the middle of the oven until the pie is baked, about 45 minutes. Cover surface with foil if it gets too dark.

🌿 Allow the pie to cool and dust it with powdered sugar before serving. Serve with berries and vanilla ice cream.

LEMON CHEESECAKE WITH VODKA-SPIKED BERRIES

4 Servings

2 eggs
1/4 cup granulated sugar
zest and juice from 1 lemon
8.8 oz. cottage cheese
2 tbsp. flour
1/2 cup plus 2 tbsp. milk, 2 percent

Serve with
vodka-spiked berries

It is easy and totally hassle-free to bake a cheesecake using cottage cheese. I like to use individual baking molds; it is both festive and more dessertlike, but a larger baking pan will do just fine. Remember to increase the baking time if you choose the latter.

🌿 Preheat the oven to 325°F. Grease four individual baking molds.

🌿 Whisk eggs and sugar. Add lemon zest and juice, cottage cheese, flour, and milk.

🌿 Distribute the batter into the baking molds and bake in the middle of the oven for about 30 minutes. Serve warm cheesecake with the berries.

VODKA-SPIKED BERRIES

10 oz. mixed berries such as blackberries, blueberries, raspberries, currants
3 tbsp. Explorer Lingon Blueberry or Absolut Raspberri
3 tbsp. powdered sugar

🌿 Thaw berries if they are frozen. Put them in a bowl and gently mix with vodka and sugar. Let the berries marinate about 30 minutes.

CURRANT FROMAGE

4 Servings

1 cup black currants
2 eggs
1/3 cup granulated sugar
1 cup plain yogurt
4 gelatin leaves
1 tbsp. fresh lemon juice

Fromage makes a fresh and refreshing finish to any dinner. I have made this one using yogurt. It is simply a fromage that is high in beneficial nutrients and sparse on fat. If you crave something with a higher calorie content, have an oat biscuit with vanilla with the fromage.

♣ Mix or crush the currants into a puree. Filter the mashed berries through a strainer if you want a completely smooth fromage.

♣ Separate yolks and whites. Whisk egg yolks and sugar until fluffy. Mix the egg mixture, the berry mash, and the yogurt.

♣ Soak the gelatin leaves in cold water for 5 minutes. Lift them out of the water and melt them in the lemon juice on very low heat. Stir the gelatin into the berry mix.

♣ Beat egg whites until stiff and carefully mix them into the batter.

♣ Pour the fromage into serving bowls and let it solidify in the refrigerator for at least 4 hours.

OAT BISCUIT WITH VANILLA

25–30 Pieces

5 tbsp. butter
1/3 cup granulated sugar
1/3 cup oatmeal
1/3 cup flour
1/4 tsp. baking powder
1 tsp. vanilla sugar
scant 2 tbsp. milk
1 3/4 cups light syrup

♣ Preheat the oven to 325°F. Melt butter. Add the remaining ingredients and stir into a batter.

♣ Scatter dollops of the batter onto baking trays with parchment paper. Use about 1 teaspoon of batter for each biscuit and add 10–12 dollops of the batter onto each tray.

♣ Bake in the middle of the oven for 6–7 minutes. Let the biscuits cool slightly before you remove them from the tray.

RHUBARB PIE

Seductively succulent—that's exactly what this pie is!

Dough
1 stick plus 3 tbsp. cold butter
1 1/2 cups flour
1 tbsp. powdered sugar
1 1/2 tbsp. water

Filling
about 10 oz. of rhubarb
3 1/2 oz. almond paste
4 tbsp. butter
2 beaten eggs
1/3 cup granulated sugar
zest from 1/4 lemon

Serve with
whipped cream or vanilla ice cream

❧ Use your fingers to mix butter, flour, and sugar into a crumbly mixture. Add water and knead into a smooth dough.

❧ Press the dough into a pie dish with a low rim, about 10 inches in diameter. Prick the bottom with a fork and let it stand in the refrigerator for at least 1 hour.

❧ Preheat the oven to 400°F. Chop the rhubarb into thin strips; peel it if it is rough. Grate the almond paste coarsely.

❧ Melt the butter. Whisk the eggs. Stir eggs and sugar into the butter and simmer the mix into a thick cream. Whisk constantly.

❧ Remove the cream from the heat. Stir almond paste and lemon zest into the cream and allow it to cool. Stir the rhubarb into the cream.

❧ Fill the pie shell with the cream. Bake pie in the middle of the oven until it is baked and has a beautiful color, 20–25 minutes.

STRAWBERRY ELDERFLOWER PARFAIT

6 Servings

1 quart strawberries
3 tbsp. concentrated elderflower juice
2 egg yolks
3 tbsp. powdered sugar
2 egg whites
2 tbsp. granulated sugar
1 cup whipping cream

Strawberries. Taste the word. The season is short, so seize the opportunity to indulge in them as often as you can, in all shapes and forms. The oat biscuits (p. 120) are perfect with this parfait.

🍃 Mash the strawberries and mix with the juice.

🍃 Whisk egg yolks and powdered sugar until fluffy. Beat the egg whites and the granulated sugar into a white and firm foam. Whip the cream.

🍃 Mix the mashed strawberries with the egg yolks. Fold in the cream and, lastly, the egg whites.

🍃 Pour batter into a mold, cover, and freeze for at least 4 hours.

🍃 Place the parfait in the refrigerator for about 45 minutes before it is served, or in room temperature approximately 20 minutes. Turn out the parfait; it will be easier if you use a flexible knife to loosen the parfait around the edges, and if you dip the mold briefly in hot water first.

STRAWBERRIES WITH RAW CREAM

4 Servings

2 egg yolks
2 tbsp. granulated sugar
1 cup whipping cream

Serve with
fresh strawberries

A simple and delicious cream that disappears quickly. It tastes like a cross between custard, whipped cream, and ice cream. Imagine getting all those goodies at the same time—can it get any better?

🍃 Whisk egg yolks and sugar until light and fluffy. Whip the cream.

🍃 Whisk the egg foam with the whipped cream.

🍃 Put the cream in the freezer for 1 hour so that it has a crispy edge around it. Spoon out the cream and serve immediately with fresh strawberries.

VANILLA AND CINNAMON MILK

4 Servings

2 cups milk, 2 percent
1 vanilla pod
1 cinnamon stick
2 tbsp. granulated sugar

Serve with
berries

This vanilla milk is smooth and delicious.

🍃 Simmer the milk with the split and scooped-out vanilla bean, cinnamon, and sugar for 3–5 minutes.

🍃 Let the milk get cold and pick out the vanilla pod and the cinnamon stick. Place the milk in the fridge so that you allow the flavors to mature, preferably overnight.

Pie Dough
1 1/3 cups flour
1 tbsp. granulated sugar
1 stick butter
1 egg yolk
1 tbsp. cold water

Filling
about 3 cups red currants
4–5 tbsp. granulated sugar
1 tbsp. potato flour

Meringue
3 egg whites
1 cup granulated sugar

Serve with
lightly whipped cream

CURRANT PIE WITH MERINGUE

The fresh currants break nicely against the sweetness of the meringue in this scrumptious currant pie. A dollop of whipped cream is just right with it.

❧ Mix flour and sugar in a bowl. Add the butter and work into a crumbly mixture. Add egg yolk and water and knead into a smooth dough.

❧ Press the dough into a large baking pan, 11 inches in diameter. Prick the bottom with a fork. Let it stand in the refrigerator for at least 30 minutes.

❧ Preheat oven to 400°F. Prebake piecrust in the center of the oven, about 15 minutes. Lower oven temperature to 325°F.

❧ Mix the scratched currants with sugar and potato flour.

❧ Beat egg whites into a firm foam. Add half of the sugar and whisk the batter stiff. Fold in the remaining sugar.

❧ Spread currants in the pie shell and cover with the meringue batter. Bake in the middle of the oven until the meringue is lightly browned, 10–15 minutes.

STRAWBERRY SUISSE WITH LUXURIOUS CHOCOLATE SAUCE

4 Servings

Chocolate Sauce
1 cup whipping cream
1 tbsp. granulated sugar
5.3 oz. dark chocolate

Suisse
4 tbsp. slivered almonds
1 cup whipping cream
1 quart strawberries
1 quart vanilla ice cream
about 40 meringues

STRAWBERRY SUISSE WITH LUXURIOUS CHOCOLATE SAUCE

Who can resist a yummy meringue suisse? The fresh strawberries and the chocolate sauce made with real chocolate add luxury to this tasty treat.

❧ *The chocolate sauce.* Pour the cream and sugar into a saucepan. Simmer on low heat while stirring. Remove the pan from the heat. Break the chocolate into pieces and add to the cream. Stir until the chocolate has dissolved. Let the sauce cool.

❧ *The suisse.* Toast the almonds in a dry, hot skillet and shake it so that the almonds do not burn.

❧ Whip the cream. Optional: divide the bigger strawberries in half.

❧ Spread ice cream, meringues, and strawberries on a platter. Top it off with cream. Pour the chocolate sauce over and sprinkle with almonds.

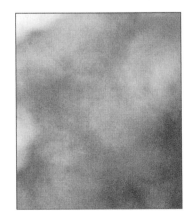

4 Servings

1 vanilla pod
2 cups whipping cream
3 tbsp. granulated sugar
1/2 cup lingonberries, fresh or frozen
2 gelatin sheets

LINGON PANNA COTTA

This is a classic dessert flavored with vanilla. The lingonberries add a refreshing and pleasant flavor contrast. So simple to make and absolutely delicious to eat!

🍃 Split the vanilla bean lengthwise. Scrape the seeds into a saucepan and add the pod, too.

🍃 Add cream, sugar, and lingonberries into the pan. Simmer on low heat about 15 minutes, stirring occasionally. Lift out the vanilla pod.

🍃 Soak the gelatin sheets in cold water for 5 minutes. Lift the sheets out, add them to the cream blend, and stir until dissolved.

🍃 Pour the mixture into four glasses or cups. Allow the panna cotta to solidify in the refrigerator for at least 4 hours before serving it.

3 1/2 cups mixed berries, such as
raspberries, blackberries, blueberries,
and cloudberries
5 tbsp. raw sugar
zest from 1 lemon
4 tsp. fresh lemon juice
3.5 oz. cream cheese, room temperature
4.4 oz. cottage cheese
1 tsp. vanilla sugar
1 1/2 tbsp. liquid honey
1 egg yolk
1 egg white

Garnish With
dark chocolate

BERRY DESSERT WITH TOPPING

Marinated berries with a fluffy and creamy topping. This dessert is as easy to cook as it will be appreciated.

🍃 Mix berries, sugar, lemon zest, and juice. Distribute the berries into four glasses.

🍃 Mix cream cheese, cottage cheese, vanilla, and honey. Stir in egg yolk.

🍃 Beat the whites into solid foam. Fold into the batter.

🍃 Top the berries with the batter and slice dark chocolate over.

Bottom
14 oz. almond paste
4 eggs
4 tbsp. cocoa powder
zest from 1 orange

Mousse
10 oz. milk chocolate
4 egg yolks
2 cups whipping cream

Garnish With
fresh raspberries
dark chocolate

MILK CHOCOLATE CAKE

Whenever you invite guests over, it is good to have a nice treat that you can make ahead of time. This super yummy cake is frozen. Perfect party cake, in other words.

❧ *The bottom.* Preheat the oven to 325°F. Grate almond paste on the grater's fine side. Stir in eggs, one by one, cocoa, and orange zest.

❧ Pour the batter into a greased pan with removable bottom, about 9.5 inches in diameter. Bake in the middle of the oven for about 20 minutes. Allow the cake to cool in the pan.

❧ *The mousse.* Melt the chocolate in a water bath. Remove it from the heat and let it cool off a bit. Mix in egg yolks, one at a time.

❧ Whip the cream and fold half of it into the chocolate batter. Fold in the rest of the cream.

❧ Pour the chocolate batter over the cake. Cover and freeze the cake for at least 4 hours.

❧ Let the cake stand at room temperature for about 30 minutes before serving. Garnish with fresh berries and slice dark chocolate over it.

Pie Dough
1 cup flour
2 tbsp. cocoa powder
1 tbsp. granulated sugar
5 tbsp. cold butter
1 egg yolk
1 tbsp. cold-pressed rapeseed oil
1 tbsp. water

Filling
5.3 oz. white chocolate
2 gelatin sheets
1/2 cup milk, 2 percent
2 eggs
1 1/2 tbsp. granulated sugar
1/2 tsp. vanilla sugar
zest of half a lemon
1/2 cup whipping cream

Garnish With
strawberries

STRAWBERRY PIE WITH WHITE CHOCOLATE CREAM

White chocolate and strawberries are excellent together. Fill the pie shell with a silky chocolate cream and top it off with strawberries. Mouthwatering, right?

🌿 Chop together flour, cocoa, sugar, and butter. Mix in egg yolks and oil. Add the water and work into a smooth dough.

🌿 Press the dough into a pie dish, about 10 inches in diameter. Prick the bottom with a fork. Let the piecrust stand in the refrigerator for at least 30 minutes.

🌿 Preheat the oven to 400°F. Bake the piecrust in the center of the oven, about 15 minutes. Let it cool.

🌿 Melt the chocolate in a water bath. Soak the gelatin in cold water for about 5 minutes. Heat the milk in a saucepan. Add the gelatin leaves and let them dissolve in the milk. Add the melted chocolate and stir.

🌿 Whisk the eggs, sugar, vanilla sugar, and lemon zest. Gently fold the egg mixture into the chocolate batter. Whip cream and fold it into the mixture, little by little.

🌿 Place chocolate cream in the fridge to solidify, preferably overnight.

🌿 Fill the pie shell with chocolate cream. Garnish with strawberries and serve with extra strawberries on the side.

6 medium pears
peel and juice of 1 lemon
1 cup red port wine
1 3/4 cups water
1 cup raw sugar

Cinnamon Sauce
5 egg yolks
4 tbsp. raw sugar
3 tbsp. fresh orange juice
3 tbsp. dry white wine
1 pinch cinnamon
1/3 cup whipping cream

PORT POACHED PEARS WITH CINNAMON SAUCE

Poached pears are even yummier with port wine and lemon. The pears are served with a creamy sauce flavored with cinnamon and orange.

❧ *The pears.* Peel the pears but leave the stem on. Wash the lemon and peel it with a potato peeler and squeeze out the juice.

❧ Boil the lemon peel and juice, port wine, water, and sugar in a low, wide pan.

❧ Add the pears and cook them on low heat, covered, until tender. Use a tester to check consistency. The time varies depending on the size of the pears, variety, and maturity. Turn them a few times during the cooking time. Let them cool down in the liquid.

❧ *The sauce.* Mix all the ingredients except for the cream in a saucepan with a thick bottom. Whisk and simmer on low heat. It should turn into a thick foam but do not let it boil. It takes about 5 minutes.

❧ When the sauce is thick and creamy, remove it from the heat and continue to whisk for about 1 minute. Cool the sauce.

❧ Whip the cream and fold it into the cold sauce before serving. Serve the pears with a bit of the juice and cinnamon sauce.

PLUM COMPOTE

2.2 lb. plums
1 3/4 cups water
1 cup raw sugar
1 cinnamon stick
2 × 1 ml ground ginger
2 tbsp. potato starch

Delicious for breakfast, lunch, snack, or dessert, ice-cold milk mixed with cream is a must with this dessert, and perhaps some almond macaroons, too.

❧ Wash the plums, split them, and remove the seeds. Cut the larger plums into wedges.

❧ Boil water, sugar, cinnamon, and ginger in a saucepan. Add the plums, cover with a lid, and boil them until soft.

❧ Mix the potato starch with a little bit of cold water. Remove the pan from the heat. Add the thickener while stirring. Return the pan to the heat, quickly bring the compote to a boil, and remove from the heat.

❧ Pour the compote into a bowl and sprinkle with sugar so that the surface does not become stale. Serve the compote when it has cooled off a bit, or serve it cold.

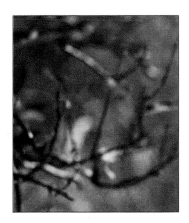 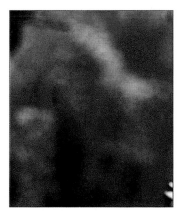  

CLOUDBERRY CHARLOTTE

Jelly Roll Cake
3 eggs
1/2 cup granulated sugar
scant 1 cup flour
1 tsp. baking powder
1 tbsp. water

Filling for the Jelly Roll
2 tbsp. cloudberry liqueur
1 cup cloudberry jam

Cloudberry Parfait
6 egg yolks
3 tbsp. granulated sugar
1 cup cloudberry jam
3 tbsp. cloudberry liqueur
2 cups whipping cream

This charlotte is a real party dessert. When it is frozen, as here, it is easy to make it in advance and just take it out from the freezer.

❧ *The jelly roll cake.* Preheat the oven to 475°F. Cover a baking sheet with parchment paper. Beat eggs and sugar until fluffy. Mix flour with the baking powder, and carefully stir it into the egg mix with water. Spread the batter over the parchment paper in an even layer.

❧ Bake in the middle of the oven for about 5 minutes. Sprinkle a little bit of sugar on the cake, cover with parchment paper, and flip the cake. Peel off the paper that the cake was baked on.

❧ Splash the cake with drops of liqueur, spread the jam over, and roll up. Wrap rolled cake in parchment paper and allow it to rest in the refrigerator for about 30 minutes.

❧ Attach a parchment paper onto the bottom of a pan with removable bottom, 26 inches in diameter. Slice the jelly roll cake. Cover the bottom and the rim of the pan with the cake slices.

❧ *The parfait.* Whisk egg yolks and sugar with an electric mixer, about 5 minutes. Stir in jam and liqueur. Whip the cream and fold into the batter.

❧ Pour the batter into the roll-cake-clad pan. Cover and let it stand in the freezer for at least 4 hours.

❧ Let the charlotte stand at room temperature for about 20 minutes before serving it. Loosen the edge of the pan and invert onto a serving plate.

BAKED

*Birthday cake made with pancakes
at home is as enjoyable as the hash
made at school was boring!
Most of us would agree that our encounters with food
serve us lasting memories.*

ROLL CAKE WITH RASPBERRY CREAM

What could be more summery than this?

🍧 Preheat the oven to 475°F. Cover a baking tray with parchment paper. Beat eggs and sugar until fluffy. Mix flour, baking powder, and vanilla sugar and stir into the water. Spread the batter evenly over the paper. Bake in the center of the oven for about 5 minutes.

🍧 Sprinkle a little bit of sugar on the cake and flip it onto parchment paper. Peel off the paper that the cake was baked on. If the paper does not come off, brush it with some water. Let it cool under the roasting pan.

🍧 Whip cream into a soft foam. Mix in raspberries and whip until the foam is stable and the berries are evenly distributed in the cream.

🍧 Spread the cream over the cake and roll it from one of the long sides. Wrap the cake in the paper and leave it with the seam down.

BERRY MUFFINS

That all berries are full of nutrients feels like a bonus. We bake, eat, and enjoy our beautiful berries because they are so heavenly good, right?

🍧 Preheat oven to 400°F. Grease and bread a muffin tin or place muffin cups on a baking tray.

🍧 Mix butter and sugar until fluffy. Add the eggs, one at a time. Mix the dry ingredients and stir them into a batter. Stir in the whipping cream.

🍧 Pour about 1/2 cup of batter into each tin or cup. Distribute the berries into the batter and press them down lightly.

🍧 Bake in the center of the oven, about 15 minutes. The muffins are done when a tester comes out clean and dry. Let the muffins cool.

🍧 Mix the ingredients for the topping. Add a dollop on top of each muffin and garnish with berries.

RHUBARB AND NUT CAKE

1 oz. walnuts
1 oz. hazelnuts
1/2 cup plus 2 tablespoons canola oil
3 tbsp. brown sugar
1 egg
1 cup flour
1/2 tsp. baking soda
1/2 tsp. baking powder
1/2 tsp. salt
2 tsp. vanilla sugar
1/2 tsp. cinnamon
1/2 cup sour cream
1 cup trimmed rhubarb,
cut into small pieces

Juicy rhubarb cake with a lot of nuts.

🦐 Preheat the oven to 325°F. Grease and flour a sponge cake pan. Chop the nuts.

🦐 Whisk the oil and the brown sugar. Add the egg and continue to whisk.

🦐 Mix the flour, baking soda, baking powder, salt, vanilla, and cinnamon.

🦐 Add flour mixture and sour cream into the batter. Lastly, add the nuts and the rhubarb.

🦐 Bake the cake on the bottom rack of the oven for approximately 50 minutes. Use a tester to make sure that it is done. Let the cake cool slightly and then turn out onto wire rack.

UNUSUAL TIGER CAKE

1 stick plus 5 tbsp. butter (room
temperature)
1 cup granulated sugar
3 eggs
scant 1 1/2 cups flour
1 tbsp. vanilla sugar
1 1/2 tsp. baking powder
zest of 1 orange
1 1/2 tbsp. orange marmalade
2 tbsp. cocoa powder
3.5 oz. coarsely chopped milk chocolate
1 tbsp. water

A tiger cake tends to tickle most people's taste buds. I bake my own version with orange and milk chocolate.

🦐 Preheat the oven to 325°F. Grease and flour a bundt cake pan.

🦐 Mix butter and sugar until fluffy. Add eggs, one at a time. Mix flour, vanilla sugar, and baking powder and fold into the batter.

🦐 Divide the batter into two bowls. Season one with orange peel and marmalade. Mix in cocoa, chocolate pieces, and water into the rest of the batter.

🦐 Spread the light batter into the pan. Drizzle the dark batter over the light.

🦐 Bake the cake on the bottom rack of the oven for 55–60 minutes. A tester should come out clean and dry when the cake is ready. Let cake cool slightly and then turn out on wire rack.

QUEEN BISCUITS IN PANS

About 48 Pieces

1 stick plus 1 tbsp. butter
2 cups milk
1.8 oz. yeast
1/2 tsp. salt
1/3 cup granulated sugar
2 tsp. freshly ground cardamom
6–6 1/3 cups flour

Filling
14 oz. thawed raspberries and blueberries
7 tbsp.. butter (room temperature)
1 cup granulated sugar

For Brushing
1 egg
crushed loaf sugar

Queen jam is a staple in many Swedish households. And what could be tastier than a lovely summer jam with raspberries and blueberries? Here the berries add flavor to the filling in these simple buns baked in pans. These biscuits tend to be popular with vanilla ice cream and fresh berries when served warm and freshly baked.

🌿 Melt the butter in a saucepan and add milk and heat until lukewarm, 98.6°F. Crumble yeast into a bowl and stir it with a little bit of the liquid. Add the rest of the liquid, salt, sugar, cardamom, and most of the flour.

🌿 Work into a smooth dough. Allow it to rise under a cloth for about 30 minutes.

🌿 Allow the thawed berries to drain thoroughly. Mix together butter and sugar for the filling.

🌿 Transfer the dough to a floured surface, knead lightly, and divide it into two equal parts. Roll out each piece into two large and thin rectangles.

🌿 Spread the butter evenly over the dough, all the way to the edges. Spread berries on top. Roll up into long rolls and press lightly. Cut the rolls with a sharp knife to about 2-inch-thick pieces. Cover two rectangular baking pans with parchment paper and place the buns inside.

🌿 Cover with a cloth and let them rise for about 30 minutes. Preheat the oven to 325°F.

🌿 Brush the biscuits with beaten egg and sprinkle with pearl sugar. Bake in the middle of the oven for 20–30 minutes. Let cool slightly before the buns are lifted out of the pan.

BERRY SQUARES

1 1/2 sticks butter
2 1/2 cups granulated sugar
4 eggs
2 1/2 cups flour
1 1/2 tsp. vanilla sugar
2 cups fresh or frozen berries, such as
raspberries or blueberries
1.8 oz. almond flakes

This recipe is probably the easiest way to whip up a tempting berry cake. In the summer, seize the luxury of baking with fresh berries, but during the rest of the year, you can enjoy this treat using frozen berries.

❧ Preheat the oven to 325°F. Line a roasting pan with parchment paper.

❧ Melt the butter and let it cool. Stir sugar, eggs, flour, and vanilla sugar into the butter. Mix into a smooth paste.

❧ Pour the batter into the pan. Spread berries and almonds on top.

❧ Bake in the middle of the oven for 30–35 minutes. Lift the cake out of the pan by pulling the edges of the paper and place it on a rack. Let it cool under the pan, and cut into squares.

about 20 cookies

LINGON COOKIES WITH OAT CRISP

1 egg
2/3 cup granulated sugar
1 stick plus 3 tbsp. melted and cooled
butter
2 cups flour
1 tsp. baking powder
1 cup lingonberry jam

Oat Crisp
2/3 cup oats
4 tbsp. butter
1/2 cup granulated sugar
1 tsp. vanilla sugar
1 tsp. cinnamon

Can it get simpler than baking bread or cookies in a roasting pan and later cutting them into squares? Here I sprinkle cinnamon-spiced oats over the jam, much like a crumb pie.

❧ Preheat the oven to 400°F. Cream the eggs and sugar. Stir the cooled butter and flour mixed with baking soda into the batter.

❧ Press the dough into a pan with parchment paper, about 8 × 12 inches. Spread jam over the dough.

❧ Mix together the ingredients for the oat crisp. Sprinkle it evenly over the cake.

❧ Bake in the middle of the oven, about 25–30 minutes. Let the cake cool before cutting it into squares.

3.5 oz. hazelnuts, about 2/3 cup
2 sticks plus 2 tbsp. butter (room
temperature)
2/3 cup granulated sugar
2 eggs
2 1/2 cups flour
1 tsp. baking powder

Filling
1/2 cup cloudberry jam

Icing
2/3 cup powdered sugar
1 1/2 tbsp. water

HAZELNUT CANAPÉS WITH CLOUDBERRIES

Cloudberries and hazelnuts add a Nordic flavor to the classic jam canapés. If you want to freeze the cakes, make them without the icing and glaze them after thawing.

❧ Preheat the oven to 425°F. Grind or chop nuts in a food processor until very fine. Mix butter and sugar until fluffy. Add eggs, one at a time, and then add the nuts, and the flour mixed with baking soda.

❧ Divide the dough into four equal parts and roll into lengths, about 16 inches long. Place them on a sheet with parchment paper.

❧ Make a lengthwise depression in the middle of each length. Fill it with jam.

❧ Bake the cakes in the middle of the oven for approximately 12 minutes.

❧ Stir together powdered sugar and water to make the icing. Drizzle it over the jam on the cooled lengths. Cut into oblique cookies that are about 1 inch wide.

About 30 Cookies

14 oz. almond paste
2 small egg whites
1.8 oz. almond flakes
3.5 oz. rhubarb or 1/2 cup fresh berries,
i.e., currants

ALMOND COOKIES

Use store-bought almond paste if you want to conjure up these delicious almond cookies quickly.

❧ Preheat the oven to 400°F. Run almond paste and egg whites in the food processor until you have a smooth mass that you can shape into small balls.

❧ Shape the mixture into small balls. Roll them in almond flakes.

❧ Cut the rhubarb into small pieces. Press a little bit of rhubarb or berries into each ball and place on sheets with parchment paper.

❧ Bake in the middle of the oven until the cookies are golden and almonds are toasted, about 12 minutes.

APPLE AND MERINGUE CAKE

8–10 Pieces

1 stick plus 3 tbsp. butter
2 apples
2 egg yolks
1 egg
1/3 cup granulated sugar
1 cup flour
1 tsp. baking powder
1 tsp. cinnamon

Meringue
2 egg whites
1/3 cup granulated sugar
3 tbsp. almond flakes

Serve with
whipped cream

Lemon and meringue pie is a favorite for many of us. But even apple pie is delicious topped with fluffy meringue.

❧ Preheat the oven to 325°F. Grease and flour a pan with a removable bottom, 9.5 inches in diameter.

❧ Melt the butter and let it cool. Peel the apples and cut them into thin wedges.

❧ Whisk yolks, eggs, and sugar until fluffy. Add butter and the flour mixed with baking soda.

❧ Pour the batter into the pan. Spread apple slices over and sprinkle with cinnamon.

❧ Beat the whites to firm foam. Add the sugar and whisk some more. Spread meringue mixture over the cake and sprinkle with almonds.

❧ Bake in the bottom of the oven for about 50 minutes. If the cake seems to be getting too dark, insert a baking tray in the upper part of the oven.

APPLE AND BLUEBERRY CAKE

8–10 Pieces

2 eggs
2/3 cup granulated sugar
1 cup flour
2 tsp. baking powder
grated rind of 1 large lemon
5 tbsp. hot water

Filling
2 apples
1 1/2 tbsp. brown sugar
1 1/2 tbsp. granulated sugar
1 tsp. freshly ground cardamom
2/3 cup blueberries

A cake-pie with both fruits and berries. You can't go wrong with a dollop of custard on top.

❧ Preheat the oven to 400°F. Grease and flour a pan with removable bottom, about 9.5 inches in diameter.

❧ Beat eggs and sugar until fluffy. Add flour mixed with baking powder and finally add the lemon peel and water while stirring.

❧ Peel and core the apples and cut them into thin wedges. Mix brown sugar, granulated sugar, and cardamom. Put the sugar mixture and the apple slices in a plastic bag and mix.

❧ Pour the batter into the pan. Spread apple slices over and sprinkle with blueberries.

❧ Bake the cake in the middle of the oven for 40–45 minutes; a tester should come out clean and dry when it is ready.

ALMOND CLAMS WITH FRESH FIGS

20 Pieces

Almond Clams
scant 1 cup flour
4.4 oz. almond paste
7 tbsp. butter
1/2 egg

Filling
5 large fresh figs
1/3 cup glogg (mulled wine)
1 1/2 tbsp. brown sugar
8.8 oz. cottage cheese
1/2 vanilla bean

This is a legendary cake with a long history. It came to Sweden in the 1500s with the German confectioners. At that time, it was a luxury that only the wealthy could afford. The original recipe is made with ground almonds, so I have simplified it by using almond paste. I gladly make this filling with figs in mulled wine during Christmastime. In the summer, it is refreshing to flavor whipped cream with lemon zest and vanilla sugar and garnish with fresh berries.

🦋 *Almond clams.* Place flour in a bowl or in a pile on the work surface. Make a hole in the middle and grate the almond paste directly into it.

🦋 Add the butter, cut into small pieces. Work into a crumbly mixture. Add the egg and work into a dough. Let it rest covered in the refrigerator at least 1 hour.

🦋 Preheat the oven to 400°F. Roll out the dough into lengths and cut them into pieces. Flatten them out with a floured thumb into round or oval ungreased baking molds.

🦋 Place the molds on a baking sheet and bake in the middle of the oven for 8–10 minutes. Turn out the molds while they are hot. Let the cookies cool and store them in airtight jars with lids.

🦋 *Filling.* Cut off the stems from the figs and cut each fig into eight wedges. Bring mulled wine and raw sugar to a boil in a saucepan. Let it cool slightly. Pour the mulled wine over the figs and let them soak for at least 1 hour.

🦋 Mix cottage cheese with vanilla seeds that have been scraped out. Fill each cookie with a dollop of the filling. Top with the figs and serve immediately.

SAFFRON TWISTS WITH FRUIT

Dough
1.8 oz. yeast
7 tbsp. butter
2 cups milk
8.8 oz. lean quark
2 bags of saffron, 0.035 oz.
1/2 cup sugar
1 1/3 cups chopped dried fruit, such as
raisins, prunes, apricots
1/2 tsp. salt
about 7 cups flour

Filling
5 tbsp. butter (room temperature)
3.5 oz. grated almond paste
zest from 1 orange
2 tsp. cinnamon

For Brushing
1 egg
almond flakes
crushed loaf sugar

There is no Christmas without saffron bread. I usually knead nuts into the dough and make an almond filling with winter flavors like orange and cinnamon.

🍃 Crumble the yeast into a bowl. Melt the butter in a saucepan. Add milk and heat it until lukewarm, 98.6°F. Dissolve the yeast in the liquid.

🍃 Add the quark, saffron, sugar, fruit, salt, and most of the flour. Work dough until it becomes shiny and smooth. Let it rise under a cloth for about 30 minutes.

🍃 Mix together the ingredients for the filling.

🍃 Transfer the dough onto a floured surface, knead lightly, and divide into two parts. Roll out each piece to an oblong cake, about 10 × 20 inches.

🍃 Spread the butter over half of the dough and fold over the unbuttered half. Cut the dough across into 1-inch-wide strips. Split the strips lengthwise, but keep them attached at the top, like a pair of pants. Twist them and make a loose knot.

🍃 Place the twists on baking trays with parchment paper and let them rise under a cloth for about 30 minutes.

🍃 Preheat the oven to 425°F. Brush the saffron breads with the beaten egg and sprinkle with almond flakes and granulated sugar.

🍃 Bake in the middle of the oven for 5–10 minutes. Let the twists cool on a rack under a cloth.

GINGERBREAD MUFFINS WITH LINGONBERRIES

1 stick plus 3 tbsp. butter (room
temperature)
2/3 cup raw sugar
2 eggs
1 1/3 cups flour
1 tsp. baking powder
1/2 tsp. cinnamon
1/2 tsp. cardamom
1/2 tsp. ground cloves
1/2 tsp. ginger
2/3 cup fresh or frozen lingonberries
mixed with 1 tbsp. flour

Toppings
quark
lingonberries
cinnamon

Lingonberries and gingerbread. Simply a perfect combination!

❧ Preheat the oven to 400°F. Grease and bread a muffin pan, where each hole can hold 2/3 cup of batter, or use individual muffin molds and place them on a baking sheet.

❧ Cream butter and sugar fluffy. Add eggs, one at a time. Mix all the dry ingredients and stir them into the batter.

❧ Mix lingonberries and flour. If the berries are frozen, they should not be completely thawed. Fold them into the batter.

❧ Pour the batter into the molds. Bake for about 15 minutes; a tester should come out clean and dry when they are ready. Let the muffins cool.

❧ Add a dollop of quark and a few lingonberries on top of each muffin and sprinkle with cinnamon.

GINGERBREAD BALLS

About 20 Balls

1/2 cup whipping cream
2 tbsp. butter
5.3 oz. dark chocolate
1/2 tsp. ground cinnamon
2 pinches cardamom
2 pinches ground ginger
2 pinches ground cloves
2 tsp. cocoa powder

Garnish
cocoa powder

Cinnamon, cardamom, ginger, and cloves are typical Christmas flavors, but they are also delicious truffle flavors.

❧ Bring the cream to a boil. Add the butter and the chocolate and let it melt on low heat.

❧ Stir in the spices. Let the batter half-solidify in the fridge so that it will be easier to handle.

❧ Shape into round balls and sift cocoa over them. Let the balls harden in the fridge.

FRUIT CRISP BREAD

32 Pieces

1 bag of mixed dried fruit, 8.8 oz.
1 1/3 cups milk, 2 percent
1 oz. yeast
1/2 tsp. salt
rounded 1/2 cup graham flour
rounded 1/2 cup cup rye flour
rounded 1/2 cup cup barley flour
about 1/2 cup bread flour

Work Surface
barley flour

Store-bought crisp bread is great, but this delicate fruit crisp bread will beat most store-bought varieties. It is excellent with a delicious ripened cheese.

🌿 Preheat the oven to 425°F. Chop the dried fruit into fine pieces.

🌿 Heat the milk until lukewarm, 98.6°F. Dissolve the yeast into the milk.

🌿 Add the salt, all the flours, and the dried fruit. Work into a smooth dough. If the dough is too loose, mix in some more flour.

🌿 Spread barley flour over the work surface. Divide the dough into 16 pieces and roll them into round balls.

🌿 Lightly roll each ball with a textured rolling pin as thinly as possible. The crisp breads should measure about 6 inches in diameter. Flour the rolling pin lightly to make it easier.

🌿 Bake the breads in the middle of the oven on a hot baking tray until they begin to darken around the edges, about 6 minutes.

🌿 Lower the oven heat to 125°F and allow the bread to continue to bake slowly with the door ajar for about 1 hour. Let cool on a rack.

DARK BREAD WITH KEFIR

1 Bread

34 oz. kefir
1 1/2 tsp. baking soda
1 cup dark syrup
1 tsp. salt
3 cups flour
1 1/3 cups graham flour
1 cup coarse rye flour
1 cup sunflower seeds
1/3 cup flaxseed
1/3 cup raisins
1/3 cup whole hazelnuts

This dark kefir loaf is filled with lots of healthy goodness. I bake this quick bread often, because it is so easy. Just mix, pour into a bread pan, and the oven will do the rest.

🌿 Preheat the oven to 400°F. Grease a bread pan or cover it in parchment paper.

🌿 Mix together kefir, baking soda, syrup, and salt in a bowl. Add all the flour, sunflower seeds, flaxseeds, raisins, and nuts. Mix well but gently.

🌿 Pour the batter into the pan and sprinkle with a little bit of flour.

🌿 Bake in the bottom of the oven, about 60 minutes.

🌿 Reduce heat to 325°F and bake for another 30 minutes. If the bread seems to be getting too dark, cover it with aluminum foil. A tester should come out clean and dry when the bread is ready.

🌿 Let the bread rest in the mold for at least five hours before you lift it out.

Dill and chive bread

Filled root vegetable bread

DILL AND CHIVE BREAD

2 Loaves

1.8 oz. yeast
2 cups water
3 tbsp. canola oil
2 tbsp. honey
2 tsp. salt
2 tbsp. mustard
1 big bunch of chopped chives
1 big bunch of chopped dill
1 3/4 cups rye flour or wheat flour
about 3 1/2 cups high protein
wheat flour

Dill, chives, and mustard may seem like unusual bread spices. But the flavors make the bread an excellent accompaniment to seafood. This bread is also delicious to toast and serve with the weekend shrimp or topped with a dollop of seafood medley. Oven-fresh dill and chive bread is also excellent in the fall at the crayfish party.

❧ Crumble the yeast in a bowl. Heat the water until lukewarm, 98.6°F. Dissolve the yeast in the water.

❧ Mix in oil, honey, salt, mustard, and chopped herbs. Add the flour and work strongly to a smooth dough. Allow it to rise under a canvas for 1 hour.

❧ Transfer the dough onto a flour-covered surface and knead it. Shape the dough into two loaves. Place them on a tray with parchment paper and sprinkle a little bit of flour on top. Let rise under a cloth for 30 minutes.

❧ Preheat the oven to 475°F. Bake loaves in the bottom of the oven for 5 minutes, lower the heat to 400°F, and continue to bake, about 30 minutes. Tap the bottom of the bread; if it sounds hollow, it is ready.

❧ Let it cool on a rack without a cloth. Serve this bread when it is freshly baked or freeze it.

FILLED ROOT VEGETABLE BREAD

40 pieces

2 cups milk
1.8 oz. yeast
3 tbsp. canola oil
2 tsp. salt
1 tbsp. honey
1 1/3 cups rye flour
about 4 cups high protein
wheat flour

Filling
3 large carrots
3 yellow onions
1 tbsp. thyme
3 tbsp. canola oil
1/3 cup chopped parsley
gourmet salt

It might not be common to fill a loaf with root vegetables, but the result is delicious and colorful—and very Swedish.

❧ Crumble the yeast into a bowl. Heat the milk until lukewarm, 98.6°F. Dissolve the yeast in the milk.

❧ Add the oil, salt, honey, and most of the flour. Knead strongly into a smooth dough. Let it rise under a cloth for 45 minutes.

❧ Peel the carrots and grate them on the coarse side of the grater. Peel and chop the onion. Sauté the carrots, onions, and thyme in oil, about 10 minutes. Mix in parsley and season with a bit of salt.

❧ Transfer the dough to a floured surface and knead it. Divide into two parts. Roll out each piece into a 1/4 inch thick cake, which measures 20 × 12 inches.

❧ Sprinkle the vegetables over and roll up like Swiss rolls. Cut each into 20 pieces. Put them into muffin molds. Let rise under a cloth for 30 minutes. Sprinkle with a little gourmet salt.

❧ Preheat the oven to 475°F. Bake in the center of the oven, about 7 minutes. Let loaves cool on a rack, under a cloth. Serve this bread when it is freshly baked or freeze it.

PRESERVED

The seasons are nature's own way
to inspire us, especially when it comes to cooking.

RASPBERRY AND CURRANT JAM

About 34 Oz.

1 quart red or white currants
1 quart raspberries
fresh juice from half a lemon
17.5 oz. jam sugar

❧ Place currants and raspberries in a saucepan and add the lemon juice. Heat the berries slowly. Cover with a lid and simmer on low heat, about 10 minutes, shaking the pan occasionally.

❧ Add the jam sugar and turn up the heat. Boil the jam uncovered, 2–3 minutes. Do the marmalade test (p. 173).

❧ Remove the pan from the heat and skim off the foam. Let the jam stand for 15 minutes, stirring a few times to even out the temperature.

❧ Pour the jam into warm and clean jars and immediately seal them with lids. It is important to pour the jam all the way up to the rim. Store in dark and cool place, or in the refrigerator.

GOOSEBERRY JAM WITH VANILLA

About 34 Oz.

2 quarts gooseberries
2 vanilla beans
1/2 cup water
21 oz. jam sugar

❧ Clean the gooseberries. Split the vanilla pods lengthwise and scrape out the seeds with a knife. Pour berries, vanilla beans, and seeds, and water into a pot. Cover with a lid and cook over low heat, about 15 minutes, shaking the pan occasionally.

❧ Follow the preparation instructions above for raspberry and currant jam.

CLOUDBERRY JAM WITH CINNAMON

About 34 Oz.

about 2 quarts of fresh or frozen cloudberries
2 cinnamon sticks
17.5 oz. jam sugar

❧ Clean the cloudberries and put them into a pot. Slowly heat the berries and cinnamon sticks in the pot. Cover and cook over low heat, 10–15 minutes, shaking the pan occasionally.

❧ Follow the preparation instructions above for raspberry and currant jam.

BLACKBERRY JAM WITH VANILLA

About 34 Oz.

2 quarts blackberries
1 vanilla pod
17.5 oz. jam sugar

❧ Clean the berries and put them in a pot. Split the vanilla pod lengthwise and scrape the seeds into the pot. Also add the vanilla pod. Slowly heat the berries. Cover and simmer on low heat, about 15 minutes, shaking occasionally.

❧ Follow the preparation instructions above for raspberry and currant jam.

Summer has so much to offer, when nature's own pantry stands in full bloom and sparks our imagination to create savory sweets from sun-ripened fruit. Homemade jam is a delicious luxury and a great way to preserve the flavors of the summer in a jar. Enjoy your jam with sautéed minipancakes, or add a dollop to your yogurt at breakfast, or even try it as a filling in cakes and tarts.

RHUBARB AND STRAWBERRY MARMALADE

About 34 Oz.

17.5 oz. rhubarb stalks
1 quart strawberries
17.5 oz. jam sugar

Rhubarb and strawberries make a delicious combination. Treat yourself to a luxurious marmalade that tastes like summer.

🍃 Wash and peel the rhubarb if it is coarse. Cut it into 1/2- to 1-inch-thick pieces. Remove the stems and leaves from the strawberries and cut them in half. If the strawberries need to be washed, do so before removing the leaves. Place rhubarb and strawberries in a pot.

🍃 Heat slowly. Cover and cook over low heat, 10–15 minutes, shaking the pot occasionally.

🍃 Add the jam sugar and turn up the heat. Boil the jam uncovered for 2–3 minutes. Do the marmalade test.★

🍃 Remove the pan from the heat and skim off the foam. Let the jam stand for about 15 minutes, stirring gently from time to time so that the temperature is evenly distributed.

🍃 Pour the marmalade into warm and thoroughly cleaned jars and immediately put on the lids. It is important that you pour the jam all the way up to the rim. Store the jam in a dark and cool place, or in the refrigerator.

PLUM MARMALADE WITH WALNUTS

Approximately 42 Oz.

3.3 lb. plums
1/2 cup water
1 cup walnuts, cut into small pieces
2.2 lb. jam sugar

Homemade marmalade is an excellent gift. Make a bit more while you are at it and pour into jars that are a good giveaway size. Don't be surprised if the empty jars are returned to you with a request to be filled.

🍃 Wash the plums and cut them. Put them in a pot with the water. Slowly heat the fruit. Cover and simmer on low heat, about 40 minutes, shaking occasionally.

🍃 Mix in the nuts towards the end of the cooking time.

🍃 Add the jam sugar and turn up the heat. Boil the jam, uncovered, for 2–3 minutes. Do the marmalade test.★

🍃 Remove the pan from the heat and skim off the foam. Let the jam stand for about 15 minutes, gently stirring from time to time to even out the temperature. Pour the marmalade into warm and thoroughly cleaned jars and immediately cover with lids. It is important that the jam is poured all the way up to the rim. Store the jam in a dark and cool place, or in the refrigerator.

Marmalade Test

★*Cool a saucer in the freezer. Scoop up some of the hot marmalade juice onto the plate and make a line in it with a spoon. If the jelly does not come together again where you made the line, it is ready. Otherwise, cook it for another 3–5 minutes. The marmalade might need to stand for a couple of days to solidify.*

Preferably use fruits and berries that are barely ripened when you cook marmalade, jam, and jelly. Then the fruit contains high levels of pectin, nature's own gelatinous substance. Overly ripe fruits and berries contain less pectin, which often causes jams, jellies, and marmalades to be too loose.

BEET CHUTNEY

About 3 Cups

17.5 oz. beets
2 apples, 10 oz.
1 lemon
1 tbsp. vinegar essence, 12 percent
1/3 cup water
1/3 cup red wine
1/3 cup raisins
1/3 cup dark syrup
1/2 tsp. salt
1 pinch pepper

Pickled beets in all their glory. It is lots of fun to make something unique out of these sweet and lovely veggies. This chutney is a delicious addition to pork and chicken.

🍃 Peel the beets and grate them on the coarse side of the grater. Peel and core the apples. Cut them into cubes. Peel the lemon with a vegetable peeler and squeeze out the juice.

🍃 Put all the ingredients into a pot, cover with a lid, and boil for 10 minutes.

🍃 Boil gently, uncovered, until the beets are just tender and the chutney has a solid consistency, about 1 hour. Stir it a few times.

🍃 Pick the lemon peel out of the pot. Pour the chutney into clean, warm jars and seal with lids. Let the chutney cool and store it in the refrigerator. It is ready to be eaten after 1–2 weeks.

CHUTNEY WITH ROOT VEGETABLES

Approximately 50 Oz.

3 carrots
2 parsnips
1/2 turnip
1/2 celeriac
2 yellow onions
1 chili
2/3 cup white wine
1 1/3 cups water
3 tbsp. apple cider vinegar
1 cup granulated sugar
5 cloves
2 tbsp. freshly grated ginger
about 1 tsp. salt
5.3 oz. soft dried apricots
1/3 cup raisins

Chutney often has the same consistency as marmalade, but the flavor usually has a bit more zing. This one, however, does not become saucelike, and the vegetables retain their tangy quality. The dried fruit, ginger, and cloves make the chutney an excellent addition to pork, chicken, game, and grilled salmon.

🍃 Peel the vegetables and weigh them; they should weigh about 2.2 pounds. Grate them coarsely on a grater or in a food processor. Transfer the grated medley into a pot. Peel and chop the onion finely. Split the chili lengthwise, remove the core and walls, and chop the chili pulp.

🍃 Bring all the ingredients to a boil and continue to cook on low heat, uncovered, for about 1 hour. Stir a few times.

🍃 Meanwhile, cut the apricots in half. Add the dried fruit midway through the cooking time.

🍃 Pour the chutney into clean, warm jars and seal with lids. Let them cool and store in the refrigerator. The chutney is ready to be eaten after 1–2 weeks.

FALL FRUIT IN A JAR

2 large apples, about 10 oz.
2 large pears, about 10 oz.
about 1 pint of plums
1 1/3 cups blackberries

The Pickle
4 cups water
1 1/3 cups granulated sugar
1 cinnamon stick
1 vanilla pod
alt. 1 ml sodium benzoate

Be sure to preserve the flavorful fruits of fall in a jar. This fruit medley is tasty with yogurt and granola, but it becomes a delicious dessert with a scoop of vanilla ice cream.

❧ Peel apples and pears and cut them into wedges. Wash the plums, halve them, and remove the pits. Cut the plums into wedges if they are big.

❧ Layer the fruits and berries in a thoroughly cleaned glass jar with a capacity of 67 ounces.

❧ Put water, sugar, and cinnamon in a saucepan. Split the vanilla pod lengthwise and scrape the seeds into the pot, but also add the pod into the mixture. Cover with a lid and boil, about 5 minutes. Add sodium benzoate into the liquid if you wish to extend the shelf life of the fall fruit.

❧ Pour the warm liquid over the fruit. It is important that all the fruits are covered in the liquid, or they will ferment. Put the lid on and leave the jar to cool. Store in the refrigerator.

Chutney and pickled berries are nice additions to a lot of dishes. The rhubarb chutney is delicious with grilled pork, pork roast, and chicken. The Nordic chutney with lingonberries is ideal with steak, meatballs, or game. Also use chutney to flavor stews, stir-fries, or sauces. The pickled and candied berries are excellent with the meat dishes that you would normally serve with jelly, puree, or jam.

RHUBARB CHUTNEY

About 2 Cups

17.5 oz. rhubarb
2 yellow onions
2 garlic cloves
1/3 cup red wine vinegar
3 tbsp. water
2/3 cup raw sugar or granulated sugar
1/2 tsp. yellow mustard seeds
2 × 1 ml ground ginger

❧ Wash the rhubarb and peel if it is coarse. Cut it into 1/2-inch-thick slices. Chop the onions and garlic.

❧ Boil vinegar, water, sugar, mustard, and ginger in a saucepan. Stir until the sugar dissolves. Mix in the rhubarb, onion, and garlic. Simmer on low heat, uncovered, until the mixture has thickened, about 45 minutes.

❧ Pour the chutney into warm and thoroughly cleaned jars and seal with lids. Store in a dark and cool place, or in the refrigerator. The chutney is ready to be eaten after 1–2 weeks.

TANGY CURRANT COMPOTE

About 3 Cups

1 quart black or red currants
2 tbsp. apple cider vinegar or white wine vinegar
1 3/4 cups raw sugar
1/2 tsp. crushed coriander
1/4 tsp. ground cloves
1/2 tsp. ground allspice

❧ Rinse the berries and put them in a pot. Boil slowly and simmer, covered, for 10 minutes.

❧ Add the vinegar, sugar, and spices. Uncover and boil until the compote has thickened, 20–30 minutes. Stir occasionally.

❧ Pour into warm and thoroughly cleaned glass jars and seal with lids. Store the compote in a dark and cool place, or in the refrigerator. It is ready to be eaten after 1–2 weeks.

PICKLED CHERRIES

About 34 Oz.

1 quart cherries
2 bay leaves

Pickle
1 1/3 cups white wine vinegar
1/3 cup water
1 1/3 cups granulated sugar
6 allspice berries
4 cloves
1 mace
1 piece of fresh ginger

❧ Rinse the cherries and place them in clean, warm jars. Add the bay leaves.

❧ Boil vinegar, water, sugar, and spices and cook for a few minutes until the sugar has dissolved.

❧ Pour the hot pickle over the cherries and seal with a lid. Store in a dark and cool place, or in the refrigerator. The cherries are ready to be eaten after 1–2 weeks.

LIGONBERRY CHUTNEY

About 3 1/2 Cups

1 quart lingonberries
2 yellow onions
1 red chili
1 1/3 cups raw sugar or granulated sugar
1/3 cup white wine vinegar
1 cinnamon stick
1/2 tbsp. salt
1/2 tsp. cayenne pepper

❧ Peel and chop the onions. Cut the chili lengthwise, remove the seeds and walls, and chop the chili flesh finely.

❧ Mix all the ingredients in a saucepan and cook over low heat, uncovered, about 40 minutes.

❧ Pour the chutney into warm, meticulously cleaned jars and seal with lids. Store in a cool and dark place. The chutney will be ready to be eaten after 1–2 weeks.

SQUASH WITH BLACK CURRANT LEAVES

About 34 Oz.

2.2 lb. small squash
10–15 black currant leaves

Pickle
34 oz. water
3 tbsp. salt
2 tsp. granulated sugar
2 tbsp. dill seeds
2 tbsp. white wine vinegar

It's not only the berries that can be used in cooking out of the beautiful black currant bushes—the leaves are also full of flavor and make a wonderful condiment. Serve the squash with anything that you would normally eat with pickled veggies and fruits.

❧ Wash the squash, cut in half and then into pieces. Rinse the currant leaves.

❧ Layer the squash and currant leaves in a clean jar with a lid.

❧ Mix all the ingredients for the pickle. Stir until sugar and salt dissolve. The pickle does not need to be boiled.

❧ Pour it over the squash so that it is covered in the liquid and seal with the lid. Store in a dark and cool place, or in the refrigerator. The squash is ready to be eaten after 1–2 weeks.

CANDIED VEGETABLES

Approximately 50 Oz.

2.6 lb. squash
17.5 oz. tomatoes
2–3 yellow onions
2 garlic cloves
3 1/2 cups granulated sugar
2 tbsp. salt
1 cup white wine vinegar
2 tsp. whole white peppercorns
1 tbsp. coriander seeds

This is a beautiful preserve that goes well with a lot of things, such as a grilled steak, salmon, or chicken. Also, let the vegetables brighten everyday meatballs and sausage.

❧ Split the squash lengthwise and use a spoon to scoop out the seeds. Cut it into cubes. Chop the tomatoes coarsely. Peel and chop the onion and garlic.

❧ Put the vegetables in a pot. Add sugar, salt, vinegar, peppercorns, and coriander. Stir until everything is mixed.

❧ Cover with lid and boil slowly with lid on until the consistency thickens, about 1 hour. Stir occasionally.

❧ Pour into hot and clean jars and seal with lids. The candied vegetables are ready to be eaten in 1–2 weeks.

RASPBERRY JUICE WITH VANILLA

The days when juicing used to be a necessity in the household are long gone. Nowadays, homemade juice is a luxury.

About 34 Oz.

2 quarts of raspberries	1 1/3 cups water
1 vanilla pod	2 cups sugar per liter of drained juice

❧ Clean the berries. Split the vanilla pod lengthwise and scrape the seeds into a pot. Also add the vanilla pod and water.

❧ Add the berries, cover with a lid, and cook over low heat, about 10 minutes. Squeeze the berries against the sides of the pot so that the juice is extracted.

❧ Strain the berry mass through a straining cloth. Allow it to drain for about 30 minutes.

❧ Rinse the pot. Measure the juice and pour it into the pot. Stir in the sugar. Bring it to a boil over low heat, stirring to dissolve the sugar. Remove the foam.

❧ Pour the juice into thoroughly cleaned bottles. Fill all the way up to the top and seal with a cap or cork. Let the juice cool, and store in a dark and cool place or in the refrigerator.

PLUM JUICE WITH LEMON

Plum trees often provide an abundant harvest. Take the opportunity to make a delicious juice out of this delectable fall fruit.

About 101 Oz.

1 quart pitted plums	21 oz. sugar
three lemons	8 cups water

❧ Scrub the lemons in warm water and cut them into slices. Halve the plums, put them in a pot with lemon slices and sugar, and add water.

❧ Let everything boil and then stir to dissolve the sugar. Simmer for approximately 20 minutes. Squeeze the fruit against the sides of the pot to extract the juice.

❧ Strain the fruit pulp through a straining cloth. Allow it to drain for 30 minutes and then use a wooden spoon to squeeze out any additional juice.

❧ Pour the juice into clean bottles. Fill them all the way up to the top and seal with a cap or cork. Store in a dark and cool place, or in the refrigerator.

CHERRY LIQUEUR

About 34 Oz.

1 1/2 quarts cherries, preferably sour
1 1/3–1 3/4 cups sugar
1/2 vanilla bean
1 cinnamon stick
2 cloves
4 tbsp. crushed cherry seeds
24 oz. spirits, i.e., rum

The seeds give the liqueur a very delicious almondlike flavor.

❧ Remove the stems and prick the cherries with a clean needle. It requires a little bit of patience but is well worth it.

❧ Layer the berries and sugar in a clean jar with a lid. Add the scraped-out vanilla bean, the spices, and the spirits.

❧ Preheat the oven to 165°F. Rinse the seeds and dry them in the oven, about 30 minutes. Lightly crush the seeds in a mortar and add them to the liqueur in the jar.

❧ Let the liqueur stand for about 3 months. Strain and taste to determine if it needs more sugar.

❧ Pour into clean bottles and save for the winter, or even better, for next summer. This liqueur only gets better with time!

CLOUDBERRY LIQUEUR

About 2 Cups

1 pint of cloudberries
1 1/3 cups eau-de-vie

Syrup
1 cup powdered sugar
3 tbsp. water

Have a glass of liqueur with the coffee, or add a dash to the dessert to make it tastier. This liqueur is also a fabulous gift that will make you just as happy giving it away as it will make you receiving it. Save the berries; they are mouthwatering with vanilla ice cream.

❧ Clean the berries and put them in a meticulously clean glass jar with lid.

❧ Add the eau-de-vie and put the lid on. Let it stand for about 2 weeks. Turn the jar every now and then so that the sugar dissolves.

❧ Strain the berries. Cook syrup out of the powdered sugar and water and let it cool. Add the syrup to the liquor, little by little. Make sure that you do not add too much of it—it will not taste as good if it is too sweet.

❧ Pour the liqueur into a clean bottle and seal with a cork. Store for at least 2–3 months, but preferably for 6 months—it gets tastier with time.

INDEX